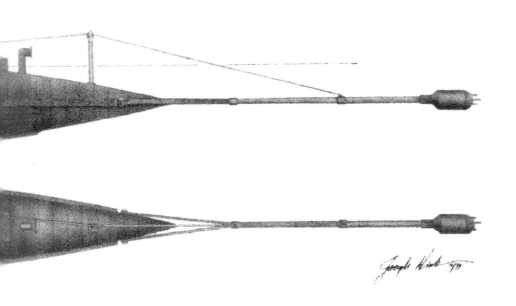

TORPEDO BOAT CSS *DAVID*

Hull: 50' - 0", Beam: 6' - 0", Draft: 4' - 6", Crew: 4, Speed: 7 knots

Spar: 20' - 7", Torpedo: 100-pound charge

Hunters of the Night

Confederate Torpedo Boats in the War Between the States

By

R. Thomas Campbell

BURD STREET PRESS

This Burd Street Press publication
was printed by
Beidel Printing House, Inc.
63 West Burd Street
Shippensburg, PA 17257-0152 USA

In respect for the scholarship contained herein, the acid-free paper used in this book meets the guidelines for permanence and durability of the Committee on Production Guidelines for Book Longevity of the Council on Library Resources.

For a complete list of available publications
please write
Burd Street Press
Division of White Mane Publishing Company, Inc.
P.O. Box 152
Shippensburg, PA 17257-0152 USA

Library of Congress Cataloging-in-Publication Data

Campbell, R. Thomas, 1937-
    Hunters of the night : Confederate torpedo boats in the War Between the States / by R. Thomas Campbell.
    p. cm.
    Includes bibliographical references and index.
    ISBN 1-57249-202-3 (alk. paper)
    1. Confederate States of America. Navy--History. 2. Torpedo-boats--Confederate States of America--History. 3. United States--History--Civil War, 1861-1865--Naval operations, Confederate. 4. Confederate States of America--History, Naval.

E596 .C363 2000
973.7'57--dc21
                                                                            00-043575

These pages are dedicated to the remembrance of the brave officers and men who designed, constructed, and crewed the Confederate torpedo boats. Their courage and determination in the face of insurmountable odds shines like a beacon through the mists of time and serves as a profound example for us all.

CONTENTS

ILLUSTRATIONS

ACKNOWLEDGMENTS

My thanks go out to the many individuals and organizations that aided me in producing these few pages. First and foremost, I must thank my wife, Carole. The fact that she tolerates my many nights at the keyboard, and then edits my work is simply amazing.

My heartfelt thanks are extended to Bob Holcomb of the Port Columbus Civil War Naval Museum, Tricia Walker of the Southern Historical Collection at the University of North Carolina, David O. Percy of the South Carolina Historical Society, Robert W. Fisch of the West Point Museum, Carolyn S. Parsons, and John Coski of the Museum of the Confederacy, and Jim Cheevers of the U.S. Naval Academy Museum.

In addition, I am indebted to Joseph Hinds of Richmond, Virginia, Phil Brigandi of Hemet, California, John E. Ellis of the Confederate States Navy Museum, Library, and Research Institute in Mobile, Alabama, as well as the kind folks at the Civil War Library and Museum in Philadelphia, Pennsylvania, and Dan Dowdey of the South Carolina State Museum. Most of all, I want to thank my publisher, White Mane, for their continued support.

INTRODUCTION

A thin cold mist had settled over the harbor of Charleston, South Carolina. There was no moon, but the twinkling of stars in an ink black sky revealed that the night was clear. A chill December wind blew from the northwest, bringing with it the putrid odor of smoldering homes and shops that had been destroyed by Union artillery shells fired indiscriminately from Morris Island. In spite of the frigid wind and the choppy water in the harbor, the Atlantic Ocean beyond Fort Sumter appeared to be relatively calm.

Lights glowed in the windows of many of the surviving old homes along the Battery, while at Atlantic Wharf down at the east end of Broad Street, sentries stomped their feet on the wooden dock in a vain attempt to stay warm. Gaslights, along with numerous torches which had been lit, illuminated a mysterious-looking vessel that was made fast to the wharf. Several Confederate sailors appeared to be preparing the vessel for immediate departure. In the flickering light of the lamps, onlookers mused among themselves that the strange bluish-colored craft resembled a huge half-submerged 50-foot cigar.

Passersby could hear steam hissing from somewhere within her bowels, and now and then wisps of gray-white smoke could be seen spiraling upward from her short stack. A bull's-eye lantern emitted a soft glow from deep within the craft while a small candle mounted in the cockpit and shielded against the wind, cast its flickering light on an ancient magnetic compass. Keen observers standing nearby noticed a long pole extending from her pointed stem, and as an occasional swell gently lifted the bow, a glistening and sinister-looking copper canister could be seen in the glow of the gaslights.

As the preparation continued, a young naval officer, looking twice his age in his smoke- and oil-stained gray uniform, paced slowly back and forth on the wharf above the boat. Occasionally, a treasured pocket watch was withdrawn from his vest, and with the strike of a match, the time was checked. It was imperative, he knew, that they not depart until the ebb tide began to flow.

When the desired time arrived, the officer stopped his pacing and spoke a soft command. Two crewmen saluted and clambered aboard. They quickly disappeared below, one forward, one aft. A third crew member, a civilian pilot, took his position at the wheel in the open cockpit just behind the funnel. The naval officer followed and began winding the winch to test the lowering and raising of the deadly canister of powder attached to the forward spar. Satisfied that the mechanism was in working order, he gingerly reeled up the torpedo, being careful to hold the latch open in order to reduce the noise of the ratchet.

With a silent nod from the officer, the pilot opened two sea-cocks and water began flooding into the ballast tanks. As the strange vessel began settling, soldiers on the wharf cast off the lines and within minutes, with the valves now closed, only her stack and the coamings of her cockpit were visible above the surface. With a few puffs of smoke she silently steamed away into the murky darkness, while on the wharf behind, one by one, the torches and lamps were quickly extinguished. As the small assemblage slowly turned away, they breathed a silent pray for the success and safety of yet another Confederate spar-torpedo boat and her courageous crew who were, once more, headed for the enemy.

CHAPTER 1

THE INFERNAL DEVICE

On a balmy Sunday morning, July 7, 1861, the USS *Pawnee*, a 1,533-ton sloop-of-war was patrolling the pristine waters of the Potomac River just south of Washington, D.C. It had been only 11 weeks since the secession of Virginia during which time Confederate troops had erected batteries of field artillery at the mouth of Aquia Creek. These guns not only guarded the water route to the railroad which led to Richmond, but also afforded protection to those Marylanders who were desirous of crossing the river and joining

A surprisingly accurate sketch of the torpedoes encountered by the *Pawnee*

Leslie's Illustrated Newspaper, July 27, 1861

their Southern brothers in arms. Skiffs, rowboats, canoes, anything that would float, were being utilized to cross the river, and Union sailors at various observation stations on the Federal warship were instructed to keep a sharp lookout for these small boats. While no boats had been spotted, one sharp-eyed observer spied a pair of black objects floating in the water not more than two hundred yards away. Commander Stephen C. Rowan ordered the *Pawnee* stopped and dispatched Master William Budd to investigate. Budd's report, filed the following day, chronicles the first Federal encounter with Confederate torpedoes:

> The apparatus in its perfect state consisted of two large oil casks connected by 25 fathoms of 3½-inch manila line, the line being kept on top of the water by corks secured to it at intervals of 2 feet. Underneath each cask, at a distance of 6 feet, was slung an iron cylinder, 4 feet 6 inches in length and 18 inches in diameter at one end and 17 inches at the other. The fuse for igniting the combustible material contained in the cylinder was placed in the cask in the following manner: The upper end of the fuse was secured on the top and near the outer end of the cask, being protected from moisture by a square box and gutta-percha pipe following it through the aperture it was placed in. It was carefully coiled on a platform secured on the inside of the cask for the purpose of protecting it from any water that might lodge in the bottom. From the platform it entered a copper pipe that connected with a gutta-percha hose, the lower end of which was secured to the iron cylinder below. In each cask were two fuses, each about 40 feet in length. All four had been on fire. Whether they were on fire or not when I first reached them I can not say, as my first act was to throw water down the air holes that were bored in the upper stave of each cask.[1]

None could have foreseen that Sunday morning that before this terrible war was concluded, the ingenuous minds of the South would devise

The screw sloop USS *Pawnee*, one of the first warships to encounter Confederate torpedoes

a more efficient and frightening means of delivering the infernal device to the sides of the Federal warships.

* * * * *

The torpedo was not an invention of the Confederacy; however, it was the Southern nation, during the War Between the States, that first applied the underwater weapon successfully in an offensive manner. The term "torpedo" at that time was applied to any underwater or subterranean explosive device, whereas today only the self-propelled underwater missile is labeled as such, the rest being classed as mines. Even with the use of modern terminology, the various boat designs employed by the Confederates to deliver the weapon to the side of an enemy ship would still be properly classified as torpedo boats. (For simplicity's sake, the word *torpedo* will be used here to include all underwater offensive and defensive explosives used during the war.) To fully comprehend the design, construction, and deployment of these vessels, it is first necessary to understand the development of the underwater explosive that came to be known as the torpedo.

The word, devised from the Latin name for an electric ray fish whose sting numbs its prey, was first used during the American Revolution by David Bushnell to describe an underwater explosive device of his own design. Bushnell had constructed his torpedo from a wooden keg in 1773, which during the war gave rise to the satirical poem, "Battle of the Kegs." While studying at Yale University, Bushnell had become obsessed with the idea of exploding gunpowder underwater. His experiments resulted in a clever device that could be exploded while submerged utilizing a clockwork mechanism. Bushnell, after extensive testing, believed that with 150 pounds of gunpowder, he could destroy any British ship afloat. He even designed a one-man submersible to carry his device and attach it to the bottom of a man-of-war. In a letter to Thomas Jefferson, dated October 1787, Bushnell described his craft and the torpedo that it carried:

> The external shape of the submarine vessel bore some resemblance to two upper tortoise shells of equal size, joined together, the flue...of entrance into the vessel being represented by the opening made by the swells of the shells at the head of the animal. The inside was capable of containing the operator and air sufficient to support him thirty minutes without receiving fresh air. At the bottom, opposite the entrance, was fixed a quantity of lead for ballast; at one edge, which was directly before the operator, who sat upright, was an oar, for rowing forward or backward; at the other edge was a rudder for steering.
>
> An aperture at the bottom, with its valve, was designed to admit water for the purpose of descending, and two brass forcing-pumps served to eject the water within when necessary for ascending. At the top there was likewise an oar, for ascending or descending, or continuing at any particular depth. A water-gauge or barometer determined the depth of

descent; a compass directed the course, and a ventilator within supplied the vessel with fresh air when on the surface.

The entrance into the vessel was elliptical and so small as barely to admit a person. This entrance was surrounded with a broad elliptical iron band, the lower edge of which was let into the wood, of which the body of the vessel was made, in such a manner as to give its utmost support to the body of the vessel against the pressure of the water. Above the upper edge of this iron band there was a brass crown or cover, resembling a hat with its crown and brim, which shut water tight upon the iron band; the crown was hung to the iron band with hinges, so as to turn over sidewise, when opened. To make it perfectly secure when shut, it might be screwed down upon the band by the operator or by a person without.

In the fore part of the brim of the crown of the vessel was a socket, and an iron tube passing through the socket. The tube stood upright, and could slide up and down in the socket six inches. At the top of the tube was a wood screw, fixed by means of a rod which passed through the tube and screwed the wood screw fast upon the top of the tube. By pushing the wood screw up against the bottom of the ship and turning at the same time, it would enter the planks; driving would also answer the same purpose. When the wood screw was firmly fixed, it would be cast off by unscrewing the rod which fastened it upon the top of the tube.

Behind the submarine vessel was a place, above the rudder, for carrying a large powder magazine. This was made of two pieces of oak timber, large enough, when hollowed out, to contain 150 pounds of powder with the apparatus used in firing it, and was secured in its place by a screw turned by the operator. A strong piece of rope extended from the magazine to the wood screw above mentioned, and was fastened to both. When the wood screw was fixed and was to be cast off from its tube, the magazine was to be cast off likewise by unscrewing it, leaving it hanging to the wood screw. It was lighter than the water, so that it might rise up against the object to which the wood screw and itself were fastened.

Within the magazine was an apparatus constructed to run any proposed length of time under twelve hours; when it had run out its time, it unpinioned a strong lock, resembling a gun lock, which gave fire to the powder. This apparatus was so pinioned that it could not possibly move, till, by casting off the magazine from the vessel, it was set in motion.

The skillful operator could swim so low on the surface of the water as to approach very near a ship in the night without fear of being discovered, and might, if he chose, approach the stem or stern above water with very little danger. He could sink very quickly, keep at any depth he pleased, and row a great distance in any direction he desired without coming to the surface. When he rose to the surface he could soon obtain a fresh supply of air, and then, if necessary, he might descend again, and pursue his course.[2]

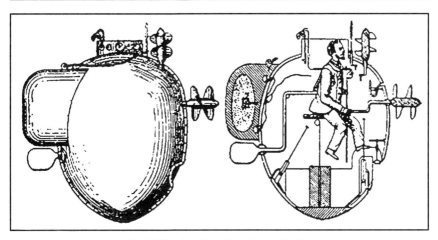

David Bushnell's *American Turtle*

Bushnell's *American Turtle*, as it was called, made three attempts to destroy a British warship in New York harbor, but for one reason or another all three were failures. After the war Bushnell preferred to live the remainder of his life in obscurity and it was Robert Fulton who took up the cause of the torpedo.

An inventive genius, Fulton at age 21 had traveled to England where he became interested in the torpedo and a means to deliver it to the enemy. Fulton felt that the possession of such a weapon would lessen the chance of naval war and reduce the risk of piracy. On October 15, 1805, Fulton demonstrated a two-man submersible of his own design to the British government. The test took place at Walmer Roads, near Deal, England. As the English dignitaries looked on, Fulton's boat, the *Nautilus*, passed beneath an old Danish brig that had been selected as the target. Following behind on a towline was Fulton's torpedo. When contact was made the torpedo exploded with a muffled roar and the old brig was blown to pieces.

Although Napoleon Bonaparte and the British admiralty expressed interest in his designs, neither nation provided wholehearted support, and as a consequence, a dejected Fulton returned to America and turned his attention to the steamboat. One reason for the lack of support, both in Europe and later in America, was that it was considered barbaric and unchivalrous to destroy one's enemy from below the surface where he had no notice of the attack or means to defend himself. By the end of the War Between the States, this Victorian notion would be dramatically shattered.

In the years leading up to the War Between the States, other countries experimented with underwater explosives. Floating mines were used by the Chinese in 1857 and 1858 at Canton and by the Russians in the Crimean

War. Not until the advent of the American war in 1861, however, were they taken seriously. One man, a Virginian, was about to prove that the torpedo was a weapon with which to be reckoned.

His name was Matthew Fontaine Maury. Renowned for his charting of the ocean currents, the scientist-sailor-oceanographer was known throughout the world as the Pathfinder of the Seas. Maury had been appointed a midshipman in the U.S. Navy at the age of 19 and over the next 36 years had attained the rank of commander during which time he had earned international recognition for his pioneering in the fields of navigation, hydrography, and meteorology. Upon the secession of his native state, Maury resigned his commission on April 20, 1861, and made his way to Richmond, Virginia, he wrote, "gave me birth; within her borders, among many friends, the nearest of kin, [and] neighbors, my children are planting their vine....In her bosom are the graves of my fathers...." Like so many others, to him this was "the path of duty and honor."[3]

Appointed by Virginia Governor John Letcher to serve on an advisory board charged with mobilizing the state's defenses, Maury was quick to realize that with few ships and numerous waterways leading into the interior of the state, a defense in the traditional sense of the word was next to impossible. Instead, Maury proposed mining the rivers and streams with torpedoes. To perfect his ideas he accepted an invitation to stay in the home of his cousin, Robert H. Maury, on Clay Street not far from where the President and Mrs. Davis had just taken up residence. There he proceeded to alarm the neighbors, by exploding small charges of powder in a washtub filled with water, splashing the walls and furniture much to the consternation of his cousin. Satisfied that his experiments would be equally successful on a larger scale, he contracted with Talbott & Son on Cary Street to build a large waterproof oak cask. Turning to Letcher, the governor supplied two barrels of gunpowder, and a full scale test on the James River was arranged.[4]

On a warm, sunny day in mid-June 1861, a host of dignitaries, including a reluctant Secretary of the Navy, Stephen R. Mallory, the entire Congressional Committee on Naval Affairs along with Governor Letcher and Maury's wife and children, had gathered at Rocketts Landing to witness the event. In 1903, Maury's son, Richard, recounted the event for posterity:

Governor John Letcher of Virginia
National Archives

Commander Matthew Fontaine Maury, CSN, the "Pathfinder of the Seas"

The torpedo was a small keg of powder, weighted to sink, fitted with a trigger to explode by percussion, to be fired when in place by a lanyard. The *Patrick Henry's* gig was borrowed; Captain Maury and the writer got aboard with the torpedo, and were rowed to the middle of the channel just opposite to where the wharf of the James River Steamboat Company now is, whereon the spectators stood; the torpedo was carefully lowered to the bottom, taking great care not to strain upon the trigger, which was at full cock; the lanyard loosely held on board. The boat pulled clear, and the writer pulled the lanyard. The explosion was instantaneous; up went a column of water fifteen or twenty feet; many stunned or dead fish floated around; the officials on the wharf applauded and were convinced, and shortly after a naval bureau of "Coast Harbor and River Defense" was created, and Captain Maury placed at its head with abundant funds for the work, and the very best of intelligent, able and zealous younger naval officers for assistants.[5]

With government endorsement and ample funds now available, Maury began planning the destruction of the nearest Federal warships. Within the next several weeks Commander Maury, his commission in the Confederate Navy having been approved on June 10, had planted torpedoes with contact fuses in the James River channel opposite Chaffin's Bluff. Rather than continue to plant devices in the James and other Virginia waterways, trusting to chance that a Federal vessel might run into one, Maury was determined instead to take his torpedoes to the enemy.

At this time five Union warships, anchored in Hampton Roads, were successfully blockading the James River and preventing access to Norfolk. Two of the enemy's vessels were flagships, the USS *Minnesota* and the USS *Roanoke*. Maury believed that, given favorable weather and sea conditions, and with a small amount of luck, he could destroy one or more of these Federal warships. Gathering a select group of men, and admonishing everyone to keep the mission secret, Maury and his crew left Richmond by train for the short trek to Norfolk. Their route took them first south to Petersburg, then along the southern bank of the James to Suffolk and Portsmouth. On July 5, 1861, the expedition pulled into the Norfolk station. From where they detrained, it was just a few miles to Sewell's Point where the Confederates had planted batteries overlooking the Roads.[6]

Later that night and again the following night, Maury and his men attempted a reconnaissance in a small boat, but a Federal steamer which kept "flying round and round," according to the commander, kept them from plotting the exact positions of the enemy ships. On Sunday, July 7, Maury was watching the Federals through his marine glass when he noticed the church flag being raised above the United States colors. According to his daughter, Betty, who later recounted her father's comments in her diary, the Confederate commander suffered twinges of nostalgia knowing that he had bowed his head in prayer countless times under those same two banners. In spite of Maury's pangs of guilt, he assembled his crew at ten o'clock that night, and embarking in five skiffs, set out toward the enemy.

Each skiff carried a wooden cask torpedo attached to 180 feet of line. The intent was to attach two of the torpedoes to each end of the line and when released, let the tide carry them across the bows of the enemy ships. If they drifted correctly, the line would snag on the vessel's bow and the torpedoes would be swept against the sides of the ship where the tension on the line would pull the trigger causing the torpedoes—hopefully—to explode. Much depended on selecting the proper location and trusting the currents to do the rest.

To reach the release point it was necessary to row approximately three miles toward Newport News near the mouth of the James River. Maury later related to Betty that

> The night was still, clear, calm, and lovely. Thatcher's Comet was flaming in the sky. We steered by it, pulling along in the plane of its splendid trail. All the noise and turmoil of the enemy's camp and fleet was hushed. They had no guard boats of any sort, and as with muffled oars we began to near them, we heard 'seven bells' strike.[7]

Betty recounted the rest of the adventure in her own words:

> After putting the magazines under one ship, the boats...were ordered back, and Papa went with the other two to plant the magazines under the other vessel.
>
> They then rowed to some distance and waited for the explosion, but it never came. Thank God, for if it had Pa would have been hung long before now.
>
> Pa thinks he can account for the failure, and could rectify it very easily. Says he was very much struck with the culpable negligence of the enemy. That he could have gone up and put his hand on those vessels with impunity.[8]

The lack of vigilance by the Union Navy would soon change, but for the moment they were completely unaware of the attack until one of the errant torpedoes was seen adrift in Hampton Roads two weeks later. In a letter to Union Navy Secretary Gideon Welles dated July 22, Flag Officer Silas H. Stringham, commander of the U.S. Atlantic Blockading Squadron, wrote that

> Sir: I have the honor to inform the Department that by information from one of the Baltimore pilots I learned there was a suspicious object down on the Horseshoe between Old Point and the light-boat.
>
> I immediately ordered the tug *Young America* to go down and bring it up. It proved similar in form to the infernal machine at the Navy Yard in Washington, which was found in the Potomac, [This refers to the torpedo found by the USS *Pawnee* which was described at the beginning of

this chapter] having but one weight to it, however, buoyed by two water breakers very neatly fixed for that purpose.

It is now on shore by the fortress, not yet having been examined.[9]

Although Maury's daughter claimed that her father was unaware of the attack in the Potomac River, the timing and similarity of the delivery of the torpedoes leads one to suspect that he was involved. The Potomac attack was carried out by Lieutenant Beverly Kennon, Jr., but absolute proof of Maury's involvement remains shrouded in mystery. One fact is certain: Maury's family, including Betty, disapproved of his activities, claiming that this was an uncivilized way to wage war against the enemy. Maury's realistic reaction was that these were invaders of his country, and that any action to destroy them was worth pursuing. In addition, he felt his actions might help to shorten the war.

Maury planned additional attacks for later in the year, but before he could carry them out the Navy Department placed him on "special duty," an assignment which greatly upset the cantankerous scientist. Mallory ordered him to New Orleans to oversee the importation of arms and ammunition from Havana, Cuba. Soon, however, Maury would abandon the idea of floating torpedoes and concentrate exclusively on the development and deployment of electrically fired explosives. In his place Mallory appointed Lieutenant Robert D. Minor to continue the projected torpedo attacks in Hampton Roads.

On October 5, 1861, Captain Franklin Buchanan, who was in charge of the Office of Orders and Detail, sent a letter to Minor ordering him to the project where he was to first consult with Maury and "receive from him such instructions as will enable you to carry out his views relating to it."[10]

Lieutenant Robert D. Minor, CSN
Naval Historical Center

It took Minor only four days to organize the next sortie and on October 10, the navy lieutenant stepped aboard the CSS *Patrick Henry* off Mulberry Point Battery on the James River. On October 11, in a letter to his mentor, Commander Maury, Minor gave a full description of the effort:

Owing to an unexpected delay in the completion of the magazines, I was unable to leave Richmond before the morning of the 9th, and did not reach this ship until yesterday about 8 a.m., when I laid your plan of the intended attack on the United States ships at anchor off Newport News before Commander Tucker, who, with Lieutenant Powell, the executive officer, placed every facility at my disposal for carrying it into execution. Acting Master Thomas L. Dornin and Midshipman Alexander M. Mason having volunteered to accompany me, the evening was passed in preparing the magazines and in explaining in detail to the officers the manner of handling and working them. In filling the tanks I found that I would have 392 pounds of powder to operate with, instead of 400, which I had calculated upon, and to insure them from sinking, I had some cork attached to the buoys, which subsequently proved of great advantage. The day was a stormy one, with a fresh breeze from the northward, with rain and mist, well suited for our operations against the enemy.

About sunset Commander Tucker got underway from his anchorage off this place, and with lights shaded, steamed slowly down the river on a strong ebb tide, until the ships were seen ahead of us, when we came to within a mile and a half of the point, dropping the anchor with a hawser bent to it to prevent noise from the rattling of the chains. The boats were then lowered, the magazines carefully slung, buoys bent on at intervals of seven feet, and, when all was ready, the crews, armed with cutlasses, took their places and were cautioned in a few words by me to keep silent and obey implicitly the orders of the officers. Acting Master Dornin, with Midshipman Mason, took the left side of the channel, while I took the right with Mr. Edward Moore, boatswain of the ship, to pilot me. Pulling down the river some 600 or 700 yards, the boats were then allowed to drift with the rapid ebb tide, while the end of the cork line was passed over to Mr. Dornin and the line tautened by the boats palling in opposite directions. The buoys were then thrown overboard, the guard lines on the triggers cut, the levers fitted and pinned, the trip line made fast to the bight at the end of the lever, the safety screws removed, the magazines carefully lowered in the water, where they were well supported by the buoys, the slack line (3 fathoms of which were kept in hand for safety) thrown overboard, and all set fairly adrift within 800 yards of the ship and 400 yards off the battery on the bluff above the point. So near were we that voices were heard on the shore, and Mr. Moore reported a boat about 100 yards off, which, however, I did not see, being too much engaged in preparing the magazines for their service.

Pulling back a short distance and hearing no explosion we returned to the ship, which we found cleared for action and ready to cover us in the event of being attacked; and the boats had just been hoisted up when signal lights were observed flashing in the vicinity of the point with considerable rapidity, indicating a suspicion on the part of the enemy that an attack of some kind was intended. Leaving our anchorage we steamed rapidly up the river and took up our former position off this place about 12:30 o'clock at night.

On going to the crosstrees this morning two ships were seen at anchor off the point, and later in the day, when seen from Warwick River, where Commander Tucker and I went to get a better view of them, they were apparently unharmed, and I concluded that the magazines could not have fouled them, though planted fairly and in good drifting distance, and with an interval between them of some 200 feet, perhaps somewhat less, as the line became entangled slightly while playing out. I have thus minutely described to you, sir, this whole operation, believing that as its originator it would be interesting to you, and perhaps serve as a guide in the further prosecution of this mode of warfare.[11]

The CSS *Patrick Henry*

Naval Historical Center

Minor had dropped the torpedoes eight hundred yards from the nearest Union warship which Maury later calculated to be too great a distance to assure accurate delivery. The Union fleet had detected that they had been attacked, but they wrongly believed that it was some form of submersible. On October 17, 1861, Federal Admiral Louis M. Goldsborough, new commander of the North Atlantic Blockading Squadron, relayed a confidential dispatch to Navy Secretary Welles:

On the 9th an attempt, no doubt, was made by the insurgence to get an infernal machine among our shipping here [Hampton Roads], but was happily foiled by the alertness of the *Lockwood*, which they tried to cut off with two tugs engaged in the nefarious business.[12]

It was now becoming painfully evident that until a better method of delivery was devised, the best possible use of the torpedo was as a defensive weapon. Consequently for the next year or so, as the Southern nation struggled to fend of the hordes of Northern invaders, her rivers, harbors, and bayous were sewn with various type of contact and electrically detonated torpedoes. Some of these were successful—some were not. It would take the invention of an ingenious young army captain in Charleston, South Carolina, which would finally enable the Confederate Navy to take the dreaded "Infernal Machine" directly to the side of the enemy's vessels.

Chapter 2

Captain Lee's Spar Torpedo Ram

Before the War Between the States, Francis D. Lee had been a well-respected and much-sought-after architect in Charleston, South Carolina. Born into one of the city's most wealthy families in 1827, Lee found himself in 1862 a captain in the Confederate Army and serving as an engineering officer on General Pierre G. T. Beauregard's staff. At the beginning of the conflict he had assisted in the design and construction of Fort Wagner on Morris Island, the massive Southern bastion which guarded the southern approaches to Charleston harbor. Lately, however, Lee had interested himself in underwater explosives and in developing a means of delivering them to the side of an enemy vessel.

His first consideration was to develop a reliable fuse mechanism to explode the torpedo underwater. While Maury's devices had depended upon some form of lanyard which, when snagged by part of a ship, would pull a trigger, Lee set about developing a fuse that would explode the torpedo upon impact. Encouraged by General Beauregard, Lee began experimenting with the idea of a chemical-type fuse. After extensive testing, he settled upon an ingenious yet simple mechanism. It consisted of a small lead tube approximately three inches in length, the head of which was capped with a very thin hemispherical piece of metal. Inside the tube Lee carefully placed a hermetically sealed glass vial containing sulfuric acid. Between the glass vial and the inner wall of the tube, he packed a composition of chlorate of potassium, powdered sugar, and very fine rifle powder. The lower part of the tube, which was screwed into the body of the torpedo, was sealed with oiled paper and was protected against leakage by brass couplings and rubber washers. With several of these screwed into the head of a torpedo it became an extremely dangerous and formidable weapon. When contact was made with the side of an enemy vessel, the impact would dent the end cap enough to break the glass vial, releasing the acid. The sulfuric acid, acting upon the composition, would ignite the rifle powder, which in turn caused the entire torpedo to explode.

Captain Francis D. Lee, CSA, inventor and advocate of the spar torpedo

The handling of these torpedoes was extremely hazardous, but General Beauregard relates how the tubes were later ingeniously altered to reduce the risk to those deploying them:

These firing tubes or fuses were afterward modified to avoid the great risk consequent upon screwing them in place and of having them permanently attached to the charged torpedo. The shell of the latter was thinned at the point where the tube was attached, so that, under water pressure, the explosion of the tube would certainly break it and discharge the torpedo; though, when unsubmerged, the explosion of the tube would vent itself in the open air without breaking the shell. In this arrangement the tube was of brass, with a leaden head, and made water-tight by means of a screw plug at its base. Both the shell and the tube being made independently water-tight, the screw connection between the two was made loose, so that the tube could be attached or detached readily with the fingers. The mode adopted for testing against leakage was by placing them in a vessel of alcohol, under the gas exhaust of an air-pump. When no air bubbles appeared the tubes could be relied on.[1]

Once Lee had perfected his detonating mechanism, he turned his attention to the torpedo itself. Up to this time most of the contrivances had been constructed as passive devices with the expectation that they would float with the current and strike an enemy, or that a Federal vessel might pass over one causing it to explode. Lee, however, was convinced that there was a better way to take the torpedo to the enemy. With this in mind, he designed a lightweight copper cylinder, which contained between 50 and 150 pounds of powder depending upon its size. The cylinder was rounded on each end, into one of which was a recessed socket designed to fit snugly over the end of a wooden pole or spar. In addition, an iron ring was usually attached to allow the torpedo to be towed by a rope. To the other rounded end of the torpedo were screwed three or four detonating fuses.[2]

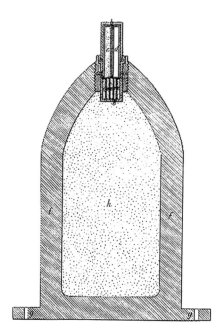

A drawing illustrating how Captain Lee's chemical fuse was inserted into the head of a torpedo.

von Sheliha: *Treatise on Coast Defence*

Lee's plan was to attach the spar to the bow of a low silhouette, high-speed steamer, which could approach an enemy warship rapidly under the cover of darkness, and

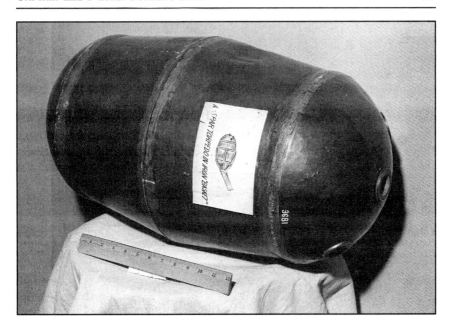

A Confederate spar torpedo now on display at the West Point Museum. Note the receptacles in the end of the device where Lee's fuses would be mounted.
West Point Museum Collections, U.S. Military Academy

ram the torpedo into her side. While the concussion from the explosion would be terrific, the young engineer was confident that the torpedo boat would be far enough away to survive the blast. During the late summer of 1862, with rolls of plans tucked under his arm, he went to see General Beauregard.

The "Creole" general had been given command of the Department of South Carolina and Georgia, relieving Major General John C. Pemberton, on August 29, 1862. Charleston was his major concern and he found the preparations for resisting an attack appalling:

> I found at Charleston an exceedingly bad defensive condition against a determined attack. Excepting Fort Moultrie, on Sullivan's Island, the works and batteries covering Charleston Harbor, including Fort Sumter, were insufficiently armed and their barbette guns without the protection of heavy traverses. In all the harbor works there were only three 10-inch and a few 8-inch Columbiads, which had been left in Forts Sumter and Moultrie by Major Anderson, and about a dozen rifle guns—unbanded 32-pounders, made by the Confederates—which burst after a few discharges.[3]

With characteristic energy, Beauregard set about to rectify the deficiencies. Troops, civilians, and rented slaves from nearby plantations labored day and night digging entrenchments, mounting cannons, cutting

General Pierre Gustave Toutant Beauregard, CSA, commander of the Department of South Carolina and Georgia. His defense of Charleston became his shining hour.

fields of fire, and transporting supplies and ammunition. All the while the commanding general kept a worried eye on the increasingly numerous Federal warships off the harbor entrance. With the Union forces growing stronger every day, he was eager to embrace any respectable plan that might contribute to the defenses of the city. It was with keen interest, therefore, that he gave his undivided attention to Captain Lee as the engineering officer unrolled his plans before him.

The drawings revealed a long, low vessel with a curved and armored turtleback deck. All that appeared above the surface was a low shield of iron, a small compartment at the stern for the pilot, and a smokestack. The crew, engine, and machinery were safely ensconced below. Protruding from the bow was a long wooden spar that could be lowered or raised by a winch operated from within. Attached to the far end of the spar was one of the captain's deadly torpedoes. Lee's plan was to approach an enemy vessel at a high rate of speed under the cover of darkness, lower the torpedo beneath the surface, and ram it into the side of the enemy ship. The resulting explosion, he felt, would blow a hole in the Federal large enough to drive a carriage through.

Beauregard was convinced, and he ordered Lee to proceed to Richmond to lay his plans before the Confederate government. Later, in his report to his commanding officer, the enthusiastic army captain reflected his bitter disappointment:

> I submitted the drawing of my torpedo and a vessel with which I propose to operate them, to the Secretary of War. While he heartily approved, he stated his inability to act in the matter, as it was a subject that appertained to the navy. He, however, introduced me and urged it to the Secretary of Navy. The Secretary of War could do nothing, and the Secretary of the Navy would not, for the reason that I was not a naval officer under his command. So I returned to Charleston without accomplishing anything.[4]

Beauregard would not be brushed off that easily. The state of South Carolina was assisting in the construction of several warships at Charleston, and on October 8, Beauregard penned a letter to Governor Francis W. Pickens. After reporting on the current state of the defensive preparations and hoping for some support from the governor, he submitted his assessment of Lee's torpedo boat:

> Capt. F. D. Lee submitted to me yesterday a plan for a torpedo ram, which I believe would be worth several gunboats. I can only express my regret it was not adopted at once by the Naval Department at Richmond when submitted to it several months ago, as he informs me. I will endeavor to have one constructed (with the authority of the War Department) as soon as materials, labor, &c., can be collected for that object. I fear not to put on record now that half a dozen of these torpedo rams, of

small comparative cost, would keep this harbor clear of four times the number of the enemy's iron-clad gunboats.[5]

Leaving no stone unturned, four days later Beauregard was writing to J. K. Sass, chairman of the State Gunboat Commission:

> Dear Sir: In view of the necessity of getting ready as soon as possible the proposed torpedo ram of Capt. F. D. Lee, and the difficulty, if not impossibility, of procuring the materials and machinery for its construction, I have the honor to request that the materials, &c., collected for the State's new gunboats should be applied to the torpedo ram, which I am informed can be got ready sooner (in less than two months), will cost less, and will be more efficacious in my opinion. In other words, I think the State and the country would be the gainers by constructing one of these new engines of destruction in place of the intended gunboat now just commencing to be built.[6]

Even though the commanding general received a pledge from Governor Pickens that the state would help finance the ram, Beauregard knew he would need help from the Confederate government in the form of materials and resources if the vessel was ever to become a reality. On October 13, 1862, he ordered Lee back to Richmond, this time with a complete set of plans, a scale model, and an introductory letter to Adjutant and Inspector General Samuel Cooper.

Lee departed Charleston that same evening, Monday, however, his journey took him longer than he anticipated. Already the Confederacy's rail system was showing the strains of war, and the young engineer was forced to take a circuitous route via Columbia and Charlotte, North Carolina. He changed trains for Raleigh, then traveled from Weldon to Petersburg, Virginia, and finally on to Richmond. At 6:30 p.m. on Thursday evening of the 16th, a weary Captain Lee alighted at the Richmond and Petersburg terminal on the corner of Byrd and Eighth Streets. His trials were only beginning.

Hiring a carriage, Lee instructed the driver to hasten to the home of William P. Miles. Beauregard had instructed Lee to look up the influential South Carolina congressman and solicit his support for the torpedo boat

Congressman William P. Miles of South Carolina
Harper's Pictorial History of the Great Rebellion

project. Miles, the former mayor of Charleston, was an excellent choice, for he was well known and respected in Richmond government circles. Upon arriving at the congressman's residence, however, Lee found Miles ill and in bed, but was requested to return the following morning. Making his way to the overcrowded Spottswood Hotel, Lee spent a restless night wondering if this trip to the Confederate capital would prove more fruitful than the last.

Early the next morning Lee, again, arrived at the Miles' residence. Although still feeling quite unwell, the South Carolina congressman ushered the young engineer into his parlor where Lee presented him General Beauregard's letter to the adjutant general:

> General: The bearer, Capt. F. D. Lee, Provisional Engineers, has submitted to me a plan of a torpedo ram for the defense of this harbor which meets my hearty approbation, as offering altogether the most practicable means of a successful encounter with the formidable ironclad gunboats of the enemy I have yet seen. This plan having been brought to the notice of the authorities of the State of South Carolina they, with their characteristic promptness, have placed at my disposition the sum of $50,000 for the immediate construction of such a ram as Captain Lee proposes. Practical builders express the belief that they can build it for the sum appropriated, but as I am aware of the difficulty of estimating with the least accuracy the cost of such work at this juncture, I have concluded to send Captain Lee to submit the details of his plan to the War Department, or, if necessary, to the Navy Department, with the hope that the cooperation of the Confederate Government may be secured, if necessary, in the construction of the one about to be begun by the State, and also that the plan will meet with such favor as to lead to the construction of similar rams for other scenes of operation. I cannot doubt that rams, properly built, according to the plan of Captain Lee would be far more effective than gunboats of the present construction, three times as large and costly, with the other important advantage of being built in one-third of the time required for rams of the present models. Time, indeed, is now of vital importance in preparing for the safety of this city and port, and should the plan which Captain Lee will submit be approved by the department and authority be given to use the materials already collected here I feel assured I can have the work done with such vigor as to have a ram ready for service in time to render signal aid in holding this fort for the Confederate States.

> Were some of these rams built at the same time in the Yazoo River they could dash out and clear the Mississippi River and aid materially in the recapture of New Orleans; and if effective here others would be equally efficient at Port Royal and Savannah and in James River. Let me bespeak for Captain Lee the consideration due to his zeal, intelligence, and capacity as a practical engineer.[7]

Miles scribbled a note of introduction to Cooper and sent Lee off alone to Mechanic's Hall on Ninth Street, headquarters of the War and Navy Departments. On the first floor of the four-story building, he found Adjutant General Cooper's office, and after a short frustrating delay, was ushered into the general's presence.

General Samuel Cooper was the highest-ranking military officer in the Southern Confederacy. Born in Hackensack, New Jersey in 1798, he married a Virginia girl in 1827, and from that moment on adopted the South as his native land. Having been graduated from West Point in 1815, Cooper proceeded to establish a distinguished career in the artillery branch of the army, seeing action in the Mexican War and against the Seminole Indians in 1841 and 1842. Ten years later he was appointed adjutant general of the United States, a position from which he resigned on March 7, 1861, to cast his lot with the Confederacy. Too old for field command, Davis appointed him to the same position in the newly formed Southern government. Well liked by both Davis and Robert E. Lee, Cooper, in addition to his many other duties, was a constant advisor on all military matters relating to the defense of the Confederacy. Into the presence of this dignified and high-ranking office stepped Captain Lee with his radical plans for a torpedo boat.

Cooper read the letter from General Beauregard and studied the plans that the engineer had spread before him. The silver-haired general listened intently as Lee explained the workings of the strange-looking vessel and the operation of the spar torpedo. Later, reporting to General Beauregard, Lee claimed that the adjutant general had received his ideas with "warm interest." Cooper was definitely impressed by the idea, and suggested that Lee submit his proposals to the secretary of war. With a crisp salute, Lee gathered his documents and rolls of plans together and followed the general's aide across the hall to Secretary George W. Randolph's office.

Unlike Cooper, the harried secretary of war had little time to spare, and after a cursory glance at Lee's plans he referred them to Colonel Jeremy F. Gilmer, chief of the Engineering Bureau. Again Lee patiently

Adjutant General Samuel Cooper, CSA, ranking military officer in the Confederacy
Harper's Pictorial History of the Great Rebellion

Confederate Secretary of War
George W. Randolph
Naval Historical Center

Colonel Jeremy P. Gilmer,
chief of the Engineering Bureau
National Archives

explained his ideas for a torpedo boat, this time to one who could understand the engineering aspects of the invention. Promising to study the drawings in detail, Gilmer asked Lee to leave the plans with him and return the following morning. It had been an exhausting day, but as he returned to his hotel, Lee was now cautiously optimistic that some form of assistance would finally be forthcoming from the Richmond government.

When the sentry unlocked the main door to the Mechanic's Hall the next morning, Captain Lee along with Congressman Miles, who was now feeling much improved, were waiting to enter. Miles was determined to cut through the red tape and immediately secured the plans and documents from Colonel Gilmer, and then led Lee directly to Secretary Randolph's office. This time the war secretary listened and observed more closely. With "warm approval" he referred the two to Secretary Mallory of the navy. Even though it was a Saturday, the building was becoming crowded with visitors as Miles and Lee climbed the long wooden staircase to the second floor which housed the Navy Department. After a short wait, they were told they could see the naval secretary.

Stephen Russell Mallory, at age 51 and a former senator from Florida, was one of the wisest choices of President Davis. Mallory, the head of the Naval Affairs Committee in the U.S. Congress for seven years, was well versed in all things pertaining to naval activities. His was a Herculean task, however, that of building a navy from practically nothing—one that could counter the strong Federal offensives that were now being aimed at Southern shores. He was, therefore, interested in any scheme that might give his fledging navy an advantage over the enemy, and he warmly received Congressman Miles and Captain Lee into his private office.

Mallory made "a careful examination of the design, expressed his deep interest in the undertaking," and much to the satisfaction of Lee and Miles, indicated "his entire willingness to furnish everything in his power to make its accomplishment as early as possible." Mallory then called Commander John M. Brooke, chief of ordnance for the navy, and John L. Porter, chief naval constructor, both of whom happened to be in the building, into his office. After reviewing the drawings and hearing Lee's explanations, they too concurred on the feasibility of the design, "as offering a valuable auxiliary to the defense of rivers and harbors."

Mallory suggested that Colonel Gilmer should again be consulted on certain technical details. Lee and Miles once more gathered the documents and descended the stairs looking for the colonel on the crowded first floor of the War Department. By the time he was located and his recommendations secured it was drawing late, and the two men left with high expectations that assistance would finally be forthcoming from the Confederate Navy. Lee was eager to return to Charleston and begin construction, so Miles promised he would return first thing Monday morning to acquire all of the needed signatures from Secretary Mallory. Lee left that night for Charleston, but he would later regret his hasty departure, which left the final negotiations in the hands of the South Carolina congressman.[8]

On October 31, Beauregard made the project official when in Special Order No. 210 from the headquarters of the Department of South Carolina and Georgia he ordered Lee to take charge of the boat's construction. Lee was given full power to "examine and supervise all accounts," and to spend the $50,000 donated by the state. The navy was to supply the engines and boilers, and Cameron & Company, machinist of Charleston, along with ship's carpenter F. M. Jones, were to do the work. While Lee was in Richmond, Constructor Porter had recommended Jones to him as "the best person to accomplish the completion of the unfinished vessel transferred by the Navy Department, inasmuch as the work, so far as it had gone, had been performed by him."[9]

The particulars concerning Captain Lee's torpedo ram are frustratingly few. Unlike many other ships of the Confederate Navy, no known contemporary drawings or photographs have survived. The sketchy accounts that are available indicate that the vessel transferred by the navy to Lee's charge was an unfinished wooden gunboat that had been abandoned on the stocks in Charleston. This may well have been a Maury designed gunboat, several of which, including the *Hampton*, and the *Nansemond*, were actually completed at Norfolk and put into Confederate service. Commander

Secretary of the Navy Stephen R. Mallory. Although Mallory was reluctant to embrace the torpedo boat, it was through his vision and determination that a Confederate Navy was created.

Mechanic's Hall on Ninth Street in Richmond, home of the War and Navy Departments

Richmond Dispatch

Maury, in addition to his torpedo experiments, had proposed the design for these boats at the beginning of the war, but while numerous contracts were given to various builders throughout the South, most were never built and the material was later diverted to the construction of ironclads. As originally conceived the Maury gunboats were approximately 110 feet in length and 20 feet in beam. They were designed to draw no more than six feet of water, which would allow them to operate on the shallow bays and estuaries of the South. The gunboat hull "abandoned" at Charleston and assigned to Lee was probably one of this design.

By November 8, 1862, the space between the ribs of the vessel had been filled in and the bow and stern had been reshaped to fit the purpose of a torpedo boat. Deck planking had begun and a large supply of pine lumber was on hand. Lee's vision of a steam driven, armored torpedo boat was off to a good start.[10]

With the verbal promise of the navy's help still fresh in his mind, Lee on November 8, optimistically dashed off a letter to Captain Duncan N. Ingraham, commandant of the navy's Charleston station:

> In compliance with our conversation of yesterday I hereby submit an estimate of some of the material which will be required for the construction of marine torpedo ram, viz, 18,500 feet oak, sawed, 4 inches thick; 6,000 pounds oakum, 5,000 pounds 8-inch spikes, one-half inch thick; 5,100 pounds 10-inch spikes, one-half inch thick; 10,500 pounds three-quarter inch iron; 4 tons of coal.[11]

In a second letter of the same day, Lee requested on behalf of Cameron & Company: "60 tons cast iron (either pig or scrap); 50 tons smith's coal; 20 tons Tennessee coke; 150 tons 2 by 7 wrought-iron bars; 10 tons 1¼ round iron for bolts; 2 tons ¼ square iron for nuts; 1 ton No. 14 sheet-iron; 1 ton No. 16 sheet-iron; one-half ton No. 12 sheet-iron; one-half ton No. 14 sheet copper; one-quarter ton No. 12 sheet-copper."[12]

That same afternoon Lee had his reply. Ingraham was very sorry, but the only items the navy had in its yard were a few three-quarter inch iron plates and a handful of eight-inch spikes. In addition, the captain noted, there was little likelihood of obtaining the supplies elsewhere. Lee

Captain Duncan N. Ingraham, CSN, commander of the Charleston station
Scharf: *History of the Confederate States Navy*

most likely now wished he had remained in Richmond and obtained Secretary Mallory's signature on documents that would have forced navy commanders to turn over construction material to him. Lee appealed to Beauregard, suggesting that perhaps the iron could be obtained from the Atlanta Rolling Mill or the Etowah Iron Works.

Meanwhile, work on the wooden portion of the hull continued. By mid-November the bow had been formed, and the design of the torpedo spar and windless had been finalized and only awaited iron for completion. Planking had begun, and Lee dispatched an agent to Richmond to see about shipping the engines, boilers, shafting, and propellers. The navy released one engine and boiler, along with a drive shaft and propeller, but Lee needed another set.

In spite of Beauregard's efforts, substantial quantities of iron failed to materialize at the construction site. Lee sent another of his agents to scour the rice plantations along the Cooper River, buying everything from parts of old cotton gins, wagon wheels, and porch railings to pots, pans, and skillets. While it was far from enough, 25 tons of scrap iron was actually collected. With no engines arriving from Richmond, notwithstanding the promise by the Navy Department, Lee wrote to Captain John McCrady, chief engineer for the state of Georgia, inquiring about the possible acquisition of the engines, shafting, boilers, and propeller of the steam tug *Barton* at Savannah. By mid-December, the purchase had been made and mechanics were dispatched to Savannah to dismantle the machinery and ship it to Charleston.[13]

Lee was now plagued by an unexpected development. Many of the carpenters and mechanics working on the vessel threatened to strike if they were not given higher wages. The Confederacy considered work stoppages as illegal, but the spiraling inflation that was beginning to grip the Southern worker was taking its toll. One cold December morning the men suddenly dropped their tools and walked off. Climbing onto a stack of lumber, Lee implored them to return, explaining that if they left their jobs they would most certainly be drafted into the army and sent immediately to the Virginia front. After talking among themselves the men grudgingly shuffled back aboard, picked up their tools, and went to work—all except one group, the free Negroes. Lee had no threats for these men. After more entreaties, however, these too, save one, joined their white comrades on the ship. John Mushington adamantly refused and walked off.[14]

By the beginning of the new year the vessel's lines were beginning to take shape. In his report to General Beauregard dated January 6, 1863, Lee reported on the progress of the torpedo ram:

> The entire hull proper of the vessel is now completed, the interior ceiling and clamping put on, and most of the deck timbers in place. The placing of the sponsings and shield will complete the ship-carpenter's portion of the work.

The workmen sent by me to Savannah have removed the boiler and engine from the *Barton*, and are taking out the bed-plate. The boiler and most of the engine have safely arrived at the Charleston and Savannah Railroad depot, and arrangements have been made to transport them to the ship-yard. After many annoying delays, Messrs. Cameron & Co. have fairly gone to work at the torpedo machinery and iron prow, of which I hope next week to report rapid progress.

Major Childs has undertaken the manufacture of the friction-tubes at the Charleston Arsenal. Captain Hartstene, C. S. Navy, has proffered me his aid in carrying the work to completion. As I am assured that his extensive nautical skill will render his services invaluable to the successful accomplishment of the work, I have at once accepted his offer. This action on my part will, I hope, meet the approval of the commanding general.

The only obstacle now in the way of the rapid completion of the work is the want of plating for armor. Everything is now ready to commence the bending of the plates as soon as they may be placed in my possession.[15]

By the end of January, all of the machinery from the *Barton* had arrived from Savannah, and the boiler had been placed in the torpedo ram. The deck was finished and the sponsings and shield were being prepared. In March, General Beauregard sent Lieutenant Colonel Alfred Roman to inspect the progress of the work, but in spite of Lee's optimistic summary, the colonel's report was not very encouraging:

Sixty-one ship-carpenters and laborers are now employed on the marine ram, under the general supervision of Capt. F. D. Lee. They work from 7 a.m. to 1 p.m. and from 2 p.m. to 6 p.m. Captain Lee and F. M. Jones, his assistant, think that the wood work of the boat will be completed in two weeks. The timber and planking for the shield is already prepared and is now being put together. The boiler and part of the engine are in place and the shafting was being fitted to the stern. The necessary repairs to the machinery (which is second-hand machinery, purchased in Savannah) are being executed at the arsenal. Captain Lee has no immediate control over that portion of the work, and he doubts whether it will be ready as soon as the rest. Both Captain Lee and Jones, being otherwise engaged, do not remain all day with the workmen. Captain Lee, however, visits the ship-yard regularly once a day.

So much time has been consumed in the building of that ram, and on the other hand the difficulty of procuring iron to shield it is so great, that no zeal, I imagine, is shown in the progress of the work. If the carpenters were ready to-day no iron could be had to complete the ram. The Navy Department has promised everything, but has given comparatively nothing. The idea of working simultaneously on four or five gunboats in Charleston instead of concentrating all the labor on one at the time is indeed so very singular that I am altogether at a loss to account for it.

From all appearance the *Palmetto State* and the *Chicora* will be the only two rams used in the defense of this harbor, whether the Federals attack us now or whether they delay it for months.[16]

On April 22, 1863, an exasperated General Beauregard angrily wrote to Adjutant General Cooper in Richmond:

The work on the marine torpedo ram is at a stand-still for want of material and money. It will be remembered that the work was undertaken with the understanding that the sum of $50,000 would be supplied by the State of South Carolina and such material as the Navy Department had available. The money has been received and is exhausted; some material has been furnished by the Navy Department, but thus far the substantial assistance of iron-plating has been denied, and hence the progress in the work has been incommensurate with its importance, and very far behind what I was led to expect when I was induced to undertake the construction.

Meantime the great value of the invention has been demonstrated so as to secure general conviction, and Captain Tucker, commanding Confederate States naval forces afloat on this station, declares unhesitatingly that this one machine of war, if finished, would be more effective as a means of defense and offense than nearly all the iron-clads here afloat and building, a fact of which I am and have been fully assured. Had it been finished and afloat when the enemy's iron-clads entered this harbor several weeks ago but few of them probably would have escaped. Be that as it may, I trust the Department will have the matter inquired into; that is, the relative value, as war engines, of the Lee torpedo ram and of the iron-clad rams *Chicora, Palmetto State*, and others of the same class now building in this harbor, to the absorption of all the material and mechanical resources of this section of the country.

I cannot express to the War Department in too strong terms my sense of the importance of the question involved and of its intimate connection with the most effective defense of this position. I do not desire to impose my views, but feel it my duty to urge an immediate investigation by a mixed board of competent officers to determine whether it be best for the ends in view to continue to appropriate all the material and employ the mechanical labor of the country in the construction of vessels that are forced to play so unimportant and passive a part as that which Captain Tucker, C. S. Navy, their commander, officially declares to me must be theirs in the future as in the past.[17]

The Creole general was indeed at his wit's end. In a letter to Colonel John Forsyth in Mobile, Alabama, on April 25, Beauregard related the status of Lee's torpedo ram "which requires only its iron plating to be ready to spread terror in the enemy's blockading fleet. Unfortunately, I cannot get the War and Navy Departments to furnish me with the necessary iron plating. I have written and telegraphed on the subject until my hand is hoarse."[18]

CHAPTER 3

ROWBOATS AT WAR

As the winter of 1862–63 progressed and the siege of Charleston ground on, it was becoming evident that Captain Lee's torpedo ram would take much longer to complete than originally anticipated. With this reality in mind, more immediate and less material extravagant means of attacking enemy vessels were proposed. One of the suggestions came directly from Secretary Mallory. On February 19, 1863, the naval secretary wrote to Lieutenant William A. Webb, currently in Richmond but about to be transferred to Charleston, suggesting an alternative method of attacking the ever-growing numbers of Federal warships off the South Carolina coast. Mallory, who understood all too well the limited ship construction capability of the Southern Confederacy, proposed a clever and well thought-out plan:

Should it be deemed advisable to attack the enemy's fleet by boarding, the following suggestions are recommended for your consideration:

First. Rowboats and barges, of which Charleston can furnish a large number.

Second. Small steamers, two or three to attack each vessel.

Third. The hull of a single-decked vessel, without spars, divided into several watertight compartments by cross bulkheads, and with decks and hatches tight, may have a deck load of compressed cotton, so placed on either side and forward and aft as to leave a space fore an aft in the center. A light scaffold, to extend from the upper tier of cotton 10 or 15 feet over the side and leading to the enemy's turret when alongside the ironclad, and over which it can be boarded at the same time that boarding would be done from forward and aft. This could be made permanent or to lower at will.

The boarders to be divided into parties of tens and twenties, each under a leader. One of these parties to be prepared with iron wedges to wedge between the turret and the deck; a second party of ten to cover the pilot house with wet blankets; a third party of twenty to throw powder down the smokestack or to cover it; another party of twenty provided with turpentine or camphene in glass vessels to smash over the turret and with inextinguishable liquid fire to follow it; another party of twenty to watch every opening in the deck or turret, provided with sulphureted cartridges, etc., to smoke the enemy out. Light ladders, weighing a few pounds only, could be provided to reach the top of the turret.[1]

Webb went to Charleston and began organizing his force. When Lee and Beauregard learned of his intentions, they suggested that as many as possible of his small boats should be equipped with a spar torpedo. Webb and others were doubtful that a small boat, such as a rowboat or skiff, could survive the blast of a torpedo a mere few feet away. Lee was convinced otherwise.

On February 27, in a letter to Brigadier General Thomas Jordan, Beauregard's chief of staff, he proposed conducting a test that once and for all would prove his theory. "I am induced to believe," he wrote, "that the entire force will be expended through the side of the vessel, for the reason that this is the only compressible substance in contact with the torpedo, the water surrounding it being perfectly noncompressible and not yielding except by actual displacement, which requires a certain lapse of time to overcome inertia of rest, a period most probably greater than will be required for the burning of a charge sufficiently great to burst in the side of the vessel."[2]

Lieutenant William A. Webb, commander of what became known as the Special Service Detachment
Library of Congress

Beauregard granted permission for the trial, and Lee secured another one of the "abandoned" gunboats, which had been loaded with debris from the "burnt district." (Charleston had experienced a devastating fire in 1861.) On March 11, with the commanding general and his staff present, Lee set out to prove his theory. Even though the hulk was heavily loaded with stones and burnt timbers, she still only drew about six and one-half feet of water. Lee was hoping for seven and one-half, but this would have to do.

The boat that Lee procured to bear the torpedo was nothing more than a frail 20-foot canoe. A long spar was suspended six feet beneath the keel of the canoe by lines running from the bow and stern, and extending approximately eight or ten feet beyond the bow. To the end of this spar Lee affixed one of his torpedoes containing a charge of 30 pounds of powder.

As the army engineer fiddled with his equipment, most observers present were convinced that if and when the torpedo exploded, the little canoe would surely be blown to pieces.

Lee's plan was to begin the experiment a 1:30 in the afternoon and a sizable crowd had gathered to watch the test. Unfortunately, the steamer, which was to tow the hulk into place, was delayed and Lee paced the dock while Beauregard and his staff waited impatiently. Finally, around 2:30 the steamer arrived and moved the hulk to the desired position, but by now a strong northwest wind was blowing. The little canoe rocked and rose with the swells and many, including Lee,

Brigadier General Thomas Jordan, Beauregard's chief of staff
Library of Congress

were concerned that the torpedo would strike the bottom and explode. The high wind also prevented the steamer from positioning the hulk broadside to Lee's proposed path of attack. With the onlookers having waited more than an hour and with General Beauregard obviously growing restless, Lee decided to attempt the test even if it meant he would have to strike the stern of the hulk.

The wind was now almost at a gale force, and it was with much difficulty that Lee finally secured a line to the bow of the canoe which he threaded through a pulley on the stern of the intended target. This line was then run back through another pulley on the stern of the canoe and then handed off to a rowboat nearby. When all was ready, Lee ordered the sailors in the rowboat to pull away. As the men in the boat strained at their oars, many on shore covered their ears and watched as the little canoe shot straight as an arrow toward the stern of the waiting hulk.

With a dull thud, the little canoe struck the stern of the old hull….But there was no explosion. Much had been made of Lee's torpedoes and now in this first public demonstration something had gone wrong. As disgruntled observers drifted away, Lee decided to leave the boat in its position against the stern of the hulk and, as he later wrote, "return to the city." Lee went on to explain that, "after giving the hands a recess of an hour, I returned to the hulk to examine the true condition of things."

Rowing to the side of the "torpedo boat," Lee gingerly backed it away from the stern of the hulk. Upon careful examination it appeared that the torpedo had just barely passed underneath the hull and none of the contact fuses had been struck. With night fast approaching the engineer secured the canoe to the side of the hulk and announced that he would conduct a new trial first thing in the morning.

The following morning, Thursday, March 12, dawned bright and clear over Charleston with only a gentle breeze now blowing out of the northwest. By 8:00 a.m., Lee was back at the test sight. There were no crowds this time. Only Captain Chisolm of Beauregard's staff, a machinist by the name of W. S. Henerey, and First Lieutenant William T. Glassell, deck officer of the ironclad CSS *Chicora*, were present. Lee again threaded his line from the torpedo boat to the hulk and back, this time with her position broadside to his direction of attack. With a wave of his arm, he signaled the men in the rowboat, and with frightening speed, the little canoe raced once more toward the waiting hulk.

A muffled thud followed quickly by a thunderous explosion ensued. Brown, muddy water bubbled to the surface as rocks, mortar, and burned timbers sailed high in the air and splashed back in the river several hundred feet away. With loud creaks and groans, the old hulk settled and was gone in less than 20 seconds. The few people who had gathered on the surrounding docks and shoreline applauded, but Lee's first concern was the condition of his canoe. Rowing up to the frail torpedo boat he found her totally uninjured. Even the wooden spar beneath the keel was still intact. Lee's theory had been proven correct. He was now confident that any vessel equipped with his torpedo could explode it against the side of an enemy ship without fear of damage to themselves.[3]

Lieutenant Glassell, who had watched the test with controlled excitement, was "now convinced that powerful engines of war could be brought into play against ironclad ships. I believed it should be our policy to take immediate steps for the construction of a large number of small boats suitable for torpedo service, and make simultaneous attacks, if possible, before the enemy should know what we were about."[4]

Although Glassell was born in Virginia, he was appointed from the state of Alabama when he entered Confederate service. He had served as a lieutenant in the United States Navy and was in China when the Southern states seceded. Returning home on board the USS *Hartford,* later to become famous as Admiral Farragut's flagship, Glassell was informed upon reaching Philadelphia on August 5, 1862, that he must take a new oath of allegiance. The young lieutenant refused because he considered the new oath inconsistent with the one that he had taken when he entered the navy. Arrested and thrown into prison at Fort Warren in Boston harbor, Glassell was confined as a prisoner of war for eight months, even though he was now a civilian and held no position in Confederate forces. Finally exchanged, he was offered a commission as a first lieutenant in the Confederate Navy, his appointment being post-dated to the same day as his incarceration. Sent to Charleston, he reported aboard the ironclad *Chicora* where he performed the duties of deck officer in charge of the first division. Glassell was on board the ironclad when she, along with the *Palmetto State*, sortied out to attack the Federal blockading fleet on January 31, 1863.[5]

Glassell immediately approached his superior, Captain Ingraham, for permission to equip 40 boats with Lee's torpedo and to be allowed to lead them against the Federal blockading fleet. He later wrote that he "offered all the arguments I could in favor of my pet hobby. Forty boats with small engines for this service, carrying a shield of boiler-iron to protect the man at the helm from rifle balls, might have been constructed secretly at one-half the cost of a clumsy ironclad."

The crusty old sea captain did not believe in what he called "new-fangled notions," and in refusing Glassell's requests, added that the lieutenant's "rank and age did not entitle him to command more than one boat," regardless of its size.[6]

Lee and Glassell, though discouraged, remained determined to prove their new weapon. With the help of financier George A. Trenholm, Glassell secured a collection of rowboats and equipped them with Lee's torpedoes, but Ingraham refused to assign the necessary officers and men. Unwilling to accept defeat, Glassell borrowed one of the cutters from the ironclad *Chicora*, and Lee attached a 50-pound torpedo to the boat in the same manner as he had the rowboat used in the sinking of the old hulk. Ingraham had not refused permission for Glassell to attack the Federals alone, so accordingly, at about 1:00 a.m. on the night of March 18, 1863, with six volunteer seamen from the *Chicora* manning the oars of the cutter, Glassell headed for the open sea.

The moon had set and the sea was calm as the lieutenant steered toward the USS *Powhatan*, whose lights were clearly visible from Fort Sumter. "The bow of the ship was toward us and the ebb tide was still running out," Glassell wrote. "I did not expect to reach the vessel without being discovered, but my intention was, no matter what they might say or do, not to be stopped until our torpedo came in contact with the ship. My men were instructed accordingly. I did hope that the enemy would not be alarmed by the approach of such a small boat so far out at sea, and that we should be ordered to come alongside."[7]

Commander William T. Glassell
Courtesy of the Orange Public Library

The USS *Powhatan* which was attacked by Lieutenant Glassell in a rowboat
Naval Historical Center

At a distance of two hundred to three hundred yards, they were discovered by the deck watch aboard the Federal vessel and ordered to halt and not come any nearer. Glassell ignored the order, and giving evasive "and stupid" answers to their questions, quietly ordered his men to pull for all they were worth. When within 40 feet of the *Powhatan*, and only seconds from striking her, one of the men, from "terror or treason," backed his oar, stopping the boat's headway. The other crewmen now gave up in despair, and the cutter drifted with the tide past the Union vessel's stern. With the *Powhatan* beginning to lower a boat to go in pursuit, Glassell drew his revolver, ordered the torpedo cut loose, and directed his men to pull away with all their strength. No shots were fired, and soon they were out of sight and headed back into the harbor.

The sailor who backed his oar, later admitted that he was terrified and now wished to make amends by accompanying Glassell on any dangerous mission. The man's shame perhaps got the best of him, for he later deserted to a Federal vessel lying at the mouth of the Edisto River. The aborted attack with the cutter, however, served to convince Glassell and Lee that steam alone would eventually be the only reliable motive power. Shortly after this, Lieutenant Glassell was ordered to Wilmington, as executive officer of the newly completed ironclad *North Carolina*, but he would soon return to Charleston. His enthusiasm for the torpedo boat was undiminished, however, and while at Wilmington he had a small steam launch equipped with a spar torpedo.[8]

In the meantime, in spite of the failure of Glassell's attack, Lieutenant Webb had managed to assemble a force of approximately 30 officers and men, in addition to renting an abandoned warehouse in which to house them. Painstakingly, he had managed to acquire an assorted collection of skiffs, canoes, a few cutters, and a depot in which to store the torpedoes. Most, but not all it appears, of the boats were fitted with 20-foot poles at the stem and upon the end of these Lee mounted his torpedoes containing 60 pounds of powder. Webb placed Lieutenant William G. Dozier in immediate charge of the various boats and on March 23, 1863, issued him specific instructions on how to best employ what had now become known as the Special Service Detachment:

> You are selected in this important expedition to carry out the design of the Navy Department, and you will be careful to preserve order and enforce strict obedience at all hazards. Be careful to select the coolest and best men under your command to discharge the torpedoes, and should the ironclads pass the batteries the first and main object is to destroy them by means of torpedoes, failing in which you will immediately board them and carry into effect the program herewith enclosed. You will keep a vigilant watch upon your leader and follow his motions, and should the boat ahead of you gain a foothold upon the first ironclad you will sheer off and attack !he next in order. After the first attack is made confusion in some degree may follow, when, I trust, your own judgment may be equal to the contest.[9]

Training of this detachment progressed rather well considering their inexperience and the hazardous occupation in which the men were involved. Soon they had lost their fear of the torpedo as evidenced by the comment of Lieutenant William H. Parker, executive officer of the ironclad CSS *Palmetto State*:

> It was not at all uncommon to see a sailor rolling down to his boat, when they were called for exercise, with a quid of tobacco in his cheek and a 60 pound torpedo stung over his back; and when it is recollected that these torpedoes had seven sensitive fuses which a tap with a stick or a blow with a stone was sufficient to explode and blow half the street down, it can readily be believed that we gave him a wide berth.[10]

Lieutenant William H. Parker, CSN
Scharf: *History of the Confederate States Navy*

Just how dangerous these torpedoes were is further illustrated by another quote from Lieutenant Parker:

> We put a torpedo on our bow (*Palmetto State*) at this time. The staff projected some 20 feet from the stem; it worked on a hinge or

gooseneck, and by means of an iron davit the staff could be raised so as to carry the torpedo out of water—when ready for use it was lowered so as to bring the torpedo about six feet under water. The torpedo was loaded with 60 pounds of rifle powder, and had screwed in it in different positions near the head seven sensitive chemical fuses. We kept it in the water ready for use, and about every two weeks would bring it on board, take out the fuses and examine the powder to see that it was dry. As executive officer I always attended to this with the gunner, and it was no joke to do it. In the first place we had to go out in a boat and take the torpedo off the staff, and in rough weather it was hard to keep the boat from striking it. As a moderate blow was sufficient to break the glass phials inside the fuses and cause an explosion, this in itself was not a pleasant occupation. Upon getting it on board we would take it on the after "fantail," (as we denominated the ends outside the shield) behind a screen, and I have passed many a *mauvais quart d'heure* while the gunner unscrewed with a wrench, and took out, all the fuses. I think it was about the most unpleasant duty I ever had to perform.[11]

After a reinforcement of a detachment of sailors from Wilmington, Dozier's force now numbered approximately one hundred men. A small steamer, the *Stono*, was assigned to act as headquarters and towboat, and the men were divided into groups of five or six depending on their respective duties. These included: "Stack Men," those given the task of dumping powder and sulfur down the smokestack of the enemy vessel; "Turretmen," whose duties included jamming the revolving turrets by driving iron wedges between the bottom of the turret and the deck of a monitor after which explosives would be poured in from the top; and "Hatch and Ventilator Men" whose assignment was to cover the hatches and other openings with wet blankets and sail cloth in an attempt to asphyxiate the crew below.

On April 9, 1863, a conference was held on board the ironclad CSS *Chicora* attended by General Beauregard, Lieutenant Webb, and Commander John R. Tucker who had recently succeeded Ingraham as commander of all Confederate forces afloat at Charleston. Numerous Federal ironclads, after undertaking an abortive and near disastrous attack on Fort Sumter on April 7, were now anchored off Morris Island. After lengthy discussions, it was decided that the Special Service Detachment would launch an attack on them the following night.

On the morning of the 10th, Parker received a signal from the flagship to report to the *Chicora*. When he arrived at the ironclad he found Commander Tucker, his hands clasped firmly behind his back, pacing the "fantail." Clambering onto the *Chicora*, Parker joined his commander who continued his pacing. "What is your opinion as to making an attack on the three upper monitors tonight with six torpedo boats?" Tucker asked. Without even breaking stride Parker answered, "I think well of it."

"Will you take the command of them?" Tucker asked.

Parker stopped dead in his tracks. Almost mechanically he responded, "Yes, Sir!" Tucker expressed his opinion that it would be advantageous to attack the three monitors lying farthest up the channel. With that an order was issued for Webb to release the boats, and Parker was given his choice of the men. As he was rowed back to the *Palmetto State*, Parker probably was thinking what he later wrote: "Now I had never had a fancy for this kind of service; in fact it was repugnant to me; but this was a case of *noblesse oblige*."[12]

Parker selected six of the best cutters including their officers and crew, but later changed his mind thinking it best to use all the boats available and attack as many of the monitors as possible. Six iron monitors in addition to the *New Ironsides*, the most powerful warship in the Federal fleet, were anchored inside the bar. Later in the day he scribbled an explanation to Webb: "After the discussion with yourself and Captain Tucker, I think it would be preferable to attack each of the enemy's ironclads now inside the outer bar with at least two of your spar torpedo rowboats instead of the number already agreed upon. I believe it to be as easy to surprise at the same time all the ironclads as a part of them."[13]

Beauregard, too, suggested that all the boats should be used. He further proposed that they should all rendezvous on the first calm night in the area behind Cummings Point, and at ebb tide coast along the beach of Morris Island just outside the surf to a point closest to the enemy's ironclads. Here Brigadier General Roswell S. Ripley would station one of his pickets who would display a light to guide them on their return. Parker's plan was to have the boats perform a hard turn to port when they reached their designated point off the beach, lower their torpedoes, and begin their attack in a line abreast. The commanding general was confident of the mission's success and wired Senators James L. Orr and Robert W. Barnwell that the expedition would "shake Abolitiondom to (its) foundation if successful."

The boat captains were instructed to attack in twos beginning with the USS *New Ironsides* and continuing on down the line to the south as opportunities arose. Each boat was expected to attack with its torpedo and sink the enemy, or failing that, the stack men, turretmen, and hatch and ventilator men were to board the enemy and smoke him out. If challenged on the approach they were to answer, "Boats on secret expedition," or "Contrabands." After the attack each boat was to head for the nearest shore using General Ripley's light as a guide. If all went as planned, they would again rendezvous behind Cummings Point.[14]

With the expedition now involving the entire detachment and all their boats, the attack was postponed until April 12. That evening, Lieutenant Parker and the boat captains held a conference in the cabin of the *Stono*, where Parker emphasized that each boat must explode its torpedo against a monitor before returning to Charleston. For those who were commanding the leaky rowboats and canoes, this must have had the overtones of a suicide order.

Fifteen boats were gathered around the *Stono*, their anxious but determined crews making last minute checks on their torpedoes, smothering devices, and additional equipment. They were all keenly aware that this would be a desperate mission. Parker detailed his plan to each boat commander. The moon would not rise, he said, until approximately 1:00 a.m.; therefore, they should time their attack so as to reach the monitors about midnight.[15]

By now darkness had settled over the *Stono* and the mass of little boats gathered around her. It was time to go. Parker shook hands with the boat captains and wished them well. Suddenly the officer of the deck announced that Commander Tucker was coming aboard. "I thought," Parker wrote, "that he had come on board to bid us 'Godspeed,' but he said as soon as he reached the deck: 'Parker, you have lost your chance— the monitors are leaving—they can be seen crossing the bar.'"[16]

By the space of a day the Special Service Detachment had missed a golden opportunity, although Parker later admitted that he had grave reservations about the mission because of the frailty of some of the boats and the inexperience of many of the crews. In fact, he wrote rather humorously that he was surprised

Commander John R. Tucker, commander of the Charleston Squadron
Scharf: *History of the Confederate States Navy*

that in the darkness they had not accidentally blown up the *Stono* or even themselves. In spite of his pessimism, however, a few of the boats were well-built cutters with experienced crews and capable captains. Given the realities of the expedition, many boats would have undoubtedly failed or turned back, but it is also probable that at least some of them would have succeeded in their attack. There would be other attempts, but never one that proffered such tantalizing possibilities of success.

The following day Beauregard suggested another plan. He proposed that four or five small steamers, burning smokeless coal, tow four torpedo boats each to the harbor entrance. When the lights of the blockading fleet could be distinguished, the torpedo boats were to be cast off and begin their attack. They were to be closely followed by the ironclads *Chicora* and *Palmetto State* whose main task was to attack and sink the *New Ironsides*. Tucker was ready to put the plan into motion when a telegram arrived from Richmond ordering the Wilmington men back to their station in North Carolina. Webb returned to Richmond and Dozier was left with 11 officers and 40 men. By April 18, the monitors had returned, but Beauregard was still hopeful, writing that "the monitors are again near here, for what purpose nothing is yet positively known. Should they come over our bar again, however, I hope that, with the row-boat spar-torpedoes I have had prepared for their reception, not one of the monitors will ever get away again."[17]

In early May several Federal monitors made a forced reconnaissance into the North Edisto River, and on May 8, Lieutenant Dozier received an order to have four boats prepared for immediate service. Parker had observed the enemy ironclads in their excursion and felt they would be vulnerable to a torpedo attack by way of Bohicket Creek. With an additional two boats borrowed from the *Chicora* and *Palmetto State*, the little flotilla left Charleston on the 10th in tow of an army tug. Their route led them up the Ashley River to Wappoo Creek, and then through this waterway into the Stono River where the boats were cast off. From there they pulled through the Wardmelaw Creek into the North Edisto.

Rather than attach the torpedoes on a spar projecting from the stem of each boat, Parker ordered them suspended beneath the keels in much the same manner as Lee's original test canoe. This was done so that they could be quickly cut away in case of an emergency. Lieutenant Glassell, who so far had avoided the order to return to Wilmington, accompanied him as second in command. The band reached White Point on the North Edisto on the night of the 10th, and the next day Brigadier General Johnson Hagood agreed to cooperate with his troops in a concerted attack on the enemy warships. That night the boats were rowed into Bohicket Creek without being detected, and hidden beneath an overgrown embankment. The crews spent the remainder of a restless night in a nearby abandoned mansion.

Early the following morning, just as the sun was beginning to break over the eastern horizon, Glassell's coxswain came up one man short on a headcount. James Murphy, the same man who had backed his oar on Glassell's attack on the *Powhatan* back in March, was missing. Scouts were dispatched in search of him, but soon a picket who had occupied the church steeple at Rockville during the night reported that about dawn he saw a boat from one of the monitors pull into the marsh and take a "stake" from it. "That 'stake' was our man," wrote Parker. "He had made a straight wake for the fleet, waded through the marsh to the water's edge and waved his hat for a boat to take him on board."[18]

With the element of surprise now gone, Parker secured several wagons and hauled the boats and men across country to the Stono River where they were launched and rowed back to Charleston via Wappoo Creek. It was a bitter disappointment. The unit strived to maintain their operational status throughout the summer, but one by one the men were transferred to other duties. By September the few that remained were distributed among the various steam torpedo boats that were nearing completion in and around Charleston, and the Special Service Detachment was disbanded. The war of the rowboats had come to an end.

CHAPTER 4

THE CSS TORCH

With the failure of the small boats, and the disbandment of the Special Service Detachment, the completion of Captain Lee's Torpedo ram was again considered. With the outer works off Charleston, Fort Sumter, Fort Moultrie, and Battery Wagner on Morris Island continually under heavy bombardment from the Federal monitors and wooden warships, it was becoming more and more imperative that they be attacked and driven off if possible. Work on Lee's torpedo boat, however, had been practically at a standstill since the end of March, but although there was no iron for her armor, her carpentry was almost finished and her machinery was in place. Now at last the navy displayed an interest in the torpedo ram. In July of 1863, Secretary Mallory sent a survey team of naval engineers to inspect the vessel to determine if she was capable of performing as intended. The engineers returned a favorable report, adding that she "would have a speed of over six knots, the same being nearly double that of the vessels now in commission in this harbor." Commander Tucker visited what was soon to be christened the CSS *Torch*, and "urged upon the Naval Department her immediate completion, and expressed the assurance that she should be far more useful than any of the ironclads in this harbor."[1]

At about this time Captain James Carlin called upon Captain Lee and offered to purchase the ram, oversee her completion, and supply his own crew. Carlin, a civilian, and an employee of the Importing and Exporting Company of South Carolina, had in 1862, commanded the blockade runner *Cecile* until she was wrecked in the Bahamas. After briefly commanding another blockade runner, the *Ruby*, he was given command of the fast new steamer *Ella and Annie* which he first ran into Charleston from Nassau on April 10, 1863. Lee listened to his proposal, but refused to sell. It is doubtful that at this time he had authority to sell the vessel anyway, but he did promise Carlin that he would be given command of the *Torch* when she became operational. Lee wrote to Beauregard stating that "Captain Carlin's full knowledge of the harbor, his cool courage and determination, all point to him as one peculiarly adapted to the proposed service, and I feel an abiding confidence that under his skillful management the torpedoes, so long unused, will yet accomplish something for the safety of this city."[2]

Lee's reputation as an engineer and ship constructor had become well known and respected in Charleston, and his work on torpedoes and the torpedo ram had not gone unnoticed. In June of 1863, the John Frazer and Company, which was responsible for much Southern shipbuilding in England in addition to their blockade-running business, offered Lee a tantalizing proposal. If he would go to England, he could supervise the construction of one of his torpedo rams and the entire cost of the vessel would be borne by the city of Charleston. Lee was eager to go and submitted the request to General Beauregard who on June 13, forwarded the application to Colonel Gilmer of the Engineering Bureau in Richmond. The authorities in Richmond said no—apparently they felt Lee was too valuable in Charleston to permit detaching him for service abroad.[3]

With the navy now actively interested and involved, construction resumed although there was as yet no iron available for the shield. In addition to the shortage of armor plates, Lee, who was still responsible for the day-to-day work, wrote that he was at a loss as to where to find the necessary funds to pay the workers. Nevertheless, on July 25, he reported that the ram would soon be ready even without her armor to "take part in any engagement."

Quietly, without fanfare or dignitaries present, the *Torch* was launched on August 1, 1863. Lee must have felt a bittersweet sense of pride as he watched her slide gracefully down the ways. The vessel was his design alone. Nothing like this had been seen before in any of the navies of the world. Yet, she was still unfinished, and it had been such a painful process to even get her this far. Still, she was at last afloat.

Immediately, however, there appeared a problem. Somehow a line from the stern of the vessel became fouled in her propeller, and she had to be hauled back into the dry dock. She was launched again the next day.

Much of the vessel was submerged with only her curved shield, pilothouse, and smokestack above water. She was painted gray in the same manner as the blockade runners which operated at night, and a "cutwater" had been added to the bow. Beauregard even suggested that spar torpedoes be attached to her sides, but this plan was never carried out. Moved to the North Atlantic Wharf, the vessel was found to be leaking badly, and 20 Negro laborers with hand pumps were hired from Adam, Damon, & Company to pump her out. After repairing the leak, and a short cruise around the harbor, which was a complete success, the navy accepted her into the Charleston Squadron and reported that she, even without her iron plating, was ready for combat.[4]

In a letter to General Jordan on August 2, Lee explained why the idea of the side torpedoes was rejected and revealed his plans for a triple torpedo warhead:

General: I am in receipt of your communication of yesterday, and would respectfully report that the additional cutwater is being prepared for the torpedo ram.

In obedience to the commanding general's instructions, I submitted the plan of attaching spar torpedoes to the sides of the vessel to Captain Carlin's consideration, and at the same time informed him of the commanding general's determination to leave the details of arrangement to his (Captain Carlin's) decision. Captain Carlin in reply expressed his preference for the use of the torpedo only in the bow of the vessel, with extra torpedoes on board, to be attached should opportunity offer for immediately renewing the attack. The reason Captain Carlin assigns is that, should he fail with his bow torpedo, the time required to swing round with the tide in order to strike with those on either side, would be ample sufficient to insure the destruction of his vessel by the enemy.

To provide against any possibility of failure in the torpedo, and to multiply the chances of success, I have proposed the use of three torpedoes in the bow, after the manner shown in accompanying sketch. Captain Carlin highly approves of this arrangement, which is now being carried into execution.[5]

Major Casper Chisolm, who was in charge of torpedoes at Boyce's Wharf, had supplied Lee with six one-hundred pound torpedoes which were carried aboard and placed under guard. While the *Torch* was now

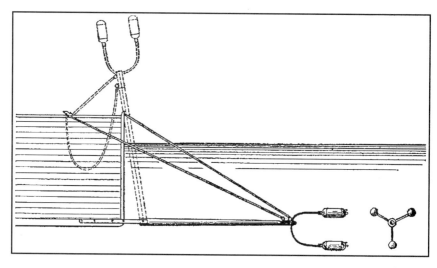

The torpedo arrangement on the bow of the CSS *Torch*

Official Records Army

afloat and operational, Lee was just about at his wit's end. While he was writing to Beauregard's chief of staff, a devastating message arrived from Commander Tucker. Lee fired off an angry letter to the commanding general the next day:

> General: I received a communication on yesterday from Capt. J. R Tucker, flag-officer, commanding afloat, stating that until he can procure officers and a crew for the torpedo-boat he will not be prepared to receive the vessel.
>
> Under these circumstances, I should be happy to receive instructions as to retaining or discharging the present crew. My difficulty is increased from the fact that there are no means at my disposal to meet present and accumulating obligations. I have written to Captain Carlin, at whose instigation the vessel was prepared for service, and who is cognizant of all the pecuniary arrangements, to take immediate steps toward a final settlement. From the evidence of every one connected with the vessel, she has exceeded, both in speed and seaworthiness, the expectations of all, and I yet hope will accomplish some important service in the defense of the city.
>
> Although feeling a regret at disconnecting myself from an enterprise which seemed to promise so much, yet I feel it a duty I owe myself and the service to respectfully request to be relieved from my present duties immediately on the adjustment of the claims now existing against the ram, and to be assigned to active duty in the field.[6]

General Beauregard, of course, refused Lee's request "for duty in the field," and encouraged the young engineer to persevere for the *Torch* was now ready to strike a blow at the enemy vessels that were pounding the Confederate positions. Captain Carlin was given command and he proceeded to form a crew of volunteers from the various vessels of the Charleston Squadron. These included: W. P. Poulnot, executive officer; Thomas Paine, pilot; James Patey, helmsman; Charles Broughton, deck hand; Thad Sims, Charles Fitzsimmons, and Veronee Charleston, engineers; John D. Clancey, and Archibald Whitney, armorers. By the third week in August, Carlin was almost ready.

One member of the crew who was indispensable was a fireman, but so far Carlin had been unable to entice any firemen from the Charleston Squadron. Someone suggested the name of Habenicht. There was only one problem—he was in jail under a sentence of death for "deserting" from Fort Sumter. In reality, a storm had prevented him from returning from leave on time, but he was sentenced to be shot anyway. Poulnot rushed to Beauregard's headquarters and asked to have the fireman released in his custody provided he, Poulnot, would accept the sole responsibility for returning him when the mission was complete. Beauregard acquiesced and wrote a note to the proper authorities, and the executive officer hurried to the local military prison. Habenicht agreed to serve saying it was probably death either way. On their way to the ship, the young fireman begged Poulnot to give him one hour to visit his family. Poulnot reluctantly agreed and the two men arranged to meet in front of the post office at a designated hour. True to his word, Habenicht walked up to Poulnot at the appointed hour and handed him a cigar. After the mission, Beauregard gladly wrote out a pardon for the young fireman.[7]

August 20, 1863, had been a hot, humid day in Charleston. All day the ground down at Battery Point, the eastern end of the city, had shook and trembled as 11 huge Union guns on Morris Island continued to send their heavy shells crashing into Fort Sumter. For four days and nights now, aided by smaller guns and the fire from the iron monitors of the Union fleet, the Federal forces had unleashed a bombardment on the Confederate fort the likes of which had never been endured in the history of warfare. Charlestonians clambered to their roofs and other places of observation and watched as the enemy shells exploded in a blinding flash against the crumbling walls of Sumter. Borne on an offshore breeze, smoke and dust drifted in over the city settling on the beautiful homes and gardens nestled along the Battery.

On this hot Thursday afternoon, as the guns rumbled in the distance and the red disk of the sun dropped behind the spire of St. Michael's church, intense activity was noted at one of the naval wharves along the Ashley River. Captain Carlin was preparing the *Torch* for a departure as soon as it became dark. Earlier, Poulnot had been dispatched to the steeple of the Orphan House to observe the positions of the Federal vessels, especially the *New Ironsides*. Passersby could hear steam hissing from the old steamboat boiler as engineers made last minute checks on the engine and various other pieces of her machinery. In the last of the fading light, a gunner from

The USS *New Ironsides*. Her upper masts, shown here, had been removed prior to her operations off Charleston.

one of the squadron's ironclads was busy making a visual inspection of the three one-hundred pound torpedoes mounted on the forward spar—any one of which could blow the largest ship out of the water. As darkness settled, oil lamps were lit below, and the small crew hurried to their assigned positions. At Carlin's command the lines were cast off, and the *Torch* steamed slowly away toward the eastern darkness of the outer harbor.

At 10:00 p.m., with the lights of Charleston twinkling in the distance, Carlin eased the torpedo boat up to the landing at beleaguered Fort Sumter. Even at this hour the fort was still under a desultory fire from Union guns mounted on Morris Island, and so moving at the double-quick, a guard of 10 soldiers, commanded by Lieutenant Eldred S. Flicking, scrambled aboard. Carlin's intent was to use these men as protection against boarders. An enemy shell exploded on the rampart nearby as Carlin quickly backed the torpedo boat away from the Sumter landing. Calling to the helmsman who was below deck, he had the ship's head swung toward the open sea, and

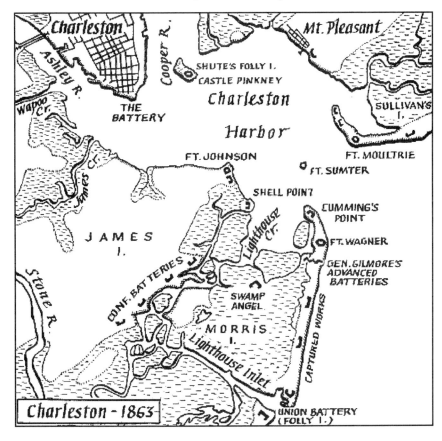

Map of Charleston Harbor

Harper's Weekly

by 11:30 p.m. the last of the obstructions and fortifications were passed—the *Torch* was now on her own.

The sea was relatively calm, with only a slight swell impeding the progress of the torpedo boat. The night was dark, for the moon had yet to rise, and the *Torch*, riding low in the water and burning anthracite coal which gave off few sparks and little smoke, was nearly invisible. Occasionally, white beams of calcium light could be seen stabbing the darkness as some Union steamer searched the sea for a suspected blockade runner. Carlin, Poulnot, and a pilot stood on deck forward of the shield. To seaward they could discern the lights of the Federal monitors where they had anchored after a long day of firing on Fort Sumter. The flickering lights farthest on the left, Carlin knew, had to be the lights of the USS *New Ironsides*, for she always anchored at the northern end of the monitors. Calling to the helmsman once more, Carlin gave a magnetic heading that pointed the bow of the *Torch* directly toward the unsuspecting enemy warship. Another order passed below brought the steam valves wide open, and the old engine from the *Barton* pounded away as the torpedo ram surged through the water toward the lights of the Federal ship.

The *Torch* was rapidly approaching the enemy from astern, and in his report to General Beauregard two days later, Captain Carlin graphically detailed minute by minute his attack upon the most dangerous warship in the Federal fleet:

> When I came within a quarter of a mile of the *Ironsides*, I lowered the torpedoes and proceeded directly for the ship, feeling at the same time fully confident of striking her in the right place. At this time she was lying across the channel and heading for Morris Island. I steered up,

The *Torch* approaches the *New Ironsides* on the night of August 20, 1863.
Courtesy of Dan Dowdey

keeping the object on our port bow, and when within forty yards from the ship I stopped the engine and ordered the helm put hard a-starboard.

I noticed the slow obedience of the ship to her helm, and again gave the order, repeating it three times. It was a moment of great anxiety and expectation, and, not doubting but I would strike her, I was obliged to attend to the proper command of the officers and men and restrain any undue excitement. In this I was ably assisted by the cool, courageous bearing of Lieutenant Flicking, who commanded the force stationed for defense. I discovered, as we ranged up alongside, that, in consequence of the *Ironsides* being in the act of swinging to the ebb, we must miss with our torpedoes, but feared that her chain cable would either ignite them or detain us alongside. In either case we must have been captured. A kind Providence, however, intervened and saved our little band from such disaster. When about fifty yards distant we were hailed, "Ship ahoy!" After deliberating whether l should not give him some warning, I felt so sure of striking him, I finally answered, "Hello!" and in an official and stern tone as possible. Another hail, "What ship is that?" I answered, almost immediately, "The steamer Live Yankee."

We were still moving slowly past the bow. I gave an order to go ahead with the engine, and was informed at the same time that the enemy was boarding us. Without looking to see whether such was the case, I gave the order to defend the ship, and got my arms ready in time to prevent the firing upon some sailors that were looking at us from the ports. I saw they were not boarding, and I immediately ordered the men to hold and not fire. They dropped immediately, showing specimen of the effect of good discipline. Just at this time he hailed again, "Where are you from?" Answered, "Port Royal." I found that we had ranged just clear of his bow, and out of danger of being boarded except by launches. I then went to the engine-room to see what was the matter, as fully two minutes had elapsed since the order had been given to go ahead. I found that the engine had caught upon the center, and, notwithstanding a continued effort for at least four or five minutes, they failed to get it started ahead. I was again hailed, "What ship is that?" Answered, "The United States steamer Yankee."

I again went to the engine-room, and by encouragement to the engineers [one can only imagine what form this encouragement took—author] found her in the act of starting. Another hail and another called me to the deck, and as none of my officers heard the question, I surmised it to be an order to come to anchor or to surrender. I answered, "Aye, aye, sir; I'll come on board." I found we were moving ahead slowly, and in two minutes must have passed out of his sight, as he commenced firing in the opposite direction. He afterward fired, sweeping the horizon, two shots passing on either side about twenty feet off.

It was my intention to attack one of the monitors, but after the experience with the engine I concluded it would be almost madness to attempt it. I therefore steered back to the city.[8]

Executive Officer Poulnot remembered the moment well.

The captain, the pilot, Lieutenant Flicking, and myself pushed the vessels apart at the bow of the torpedo boat, and picked up poles and oars, and continued shoving until too far to reach the tide then helping to separate us further. The order had been given to go ahead. The engine did not budge her. I jumped below, and Habenicht and myself succeeded with the starting bar to keep her from getting on the center. After several trials the stem was pointed to get away, and at one hundred yards from the ship we commenced throwing lumps of rosin into the furnace, using several barrels carried for this especial purpose. The smoke was so dense no one could see or scarce stand it away from our vessel. This was done to avoid capture by smaller craft. Upon getting on deck I could distinctly hear the orders to clear the decks for action aboard the *Ironsides*, boatswain's pipes, drums, and orders given. "Load! Ready! Fire!" I was amazed to see and to hear two shells from their guns. One exploded on the starboard quarter close aboard and hove considerable water on the afterdeck. The other went flying ahead of us and exploded over the starboard bow. There was a general stampede of the small vessels of the fleet. In all there were nine double shotted guns turned loose at us without effect.[9]

Ensign Benjamin H. Porter was officer of the deck on the *New Ironsides* the night of the attack, and it was he who first challenged the approaching torpedo boat. His report several days later gives an interesting prospective of the attempt as seen from the deck of the Union vessel, and collaborates Captain Carlin's description:

Sir: In obedience to your order of the 26th instant, I hereby submit to you an account of the visit of the enemy's vessels to this ship a few nights since.

At 1:00 a.m. on the morning of the 21st instant, I saw a strange vessel, sitting very low in the water and having the appearance of being a large boat, coming up astern very fast. I hailed the stranger twice, receiving for an answer to the first hail, "Aye, aye," and to the second, "I am the *Live Yankee*, from Port Royal." Beat to quarters immediately and threw up rockets. In the meantime the stranger ran rapidly past our broadside and fell athwart our bows, where we could bring no guns to beat upon her. She remained there a few minutes and then started off rapidly in the direction of Fort Moultrie. Meanwhile our chain had been slipped, and backing astern, the bow guns were fired at her, but with what effect I cannot say. From the time she was first seen until she left us not more than five minutes elapsed.[10]

The *Torch*, her engine caught on "dead-center," drifts by the *New Ironside*.
Courtesy of Dan Dowdey

Carlin, chagrined over his failure to explode the torpedoes, took his frustration out on the *Torch*. In the final paragraph of his report he angrily condemned the torpedo boat:

> General, in consequence of the tests to which I have put the ship in the two late adventures, I feel it my duty most unhesitatingly to express my condemnation of the vessel and engine for the purposes it was intended, and as soon as she can be docked and the leak stopped, would advise making a transport of her.

Beauregard was not about to give up on a project on which he had spent so much time and energy, and he convinced Carlin to remain as the vessel's commander. The day after the attack the torpedo boat was moved to the other side of the city and moored at the West Point Mill Wharf. On August 23, the commanding general wrote to the dispirited master of the *Torch*:

> Captain: Your report of operations in the attempt to destroy the *Ironsides* during the night of the 18th (20th) instant has been received. I regret exceedingly that you should have met with so many difficulties in your disinterested and praiseworthy enterprise, but I am happy to learn that you are still willing to retain the command of the torpedo ram, for I know no one to whose skill and experience I would sooner trust the boat on so bold and gallant an undertaking. I feel convinced that another trial under more favorable circumstances will surely meet with success, notwithstanding the known defects of the vessel.[11]

Francis D. Lee must have been devastated. The first real test of his spar torpedo had failed miserably, though not out of any fault of the torpedoes. He had spent so much time and energy in constructing the torpedo ram only now to see her condemned as unfit for the service for which she was designed. In addition, the secret was out. Soon Federal vessels would take extra precautions to guard against future attacks by torpedo boats.

In spite of Beauregard's optimism, and Lee's continued involvement with the *Torch*, it appears that the navy took Carlin's advice and relegated the Confederacy's first steam-driven torpedo boat to a transport for the remainder of the war. She never saw action again.

CHAPTER 5

DAVID AND GOLIATH

In the spring of 1863, on a beach adjacent to Charleston harbor, a well-to-do businessman watched an impressive and terrifying spectacle through a pair of binoculars. The USS *New Ironsides* was hurling successive salvos of 11-inch shells into Battery Wagner on Morris Island. With each explosion, sand, timbers, and debris were blown high into the air, while dust and black smoke hung like a pall of death over the Confederate bastion. The man observing the bombardment was a Charlestonian named Theodore D. Stoney. What he saw through his glasses filled him with alarm. Steaming slowly less than a thousand yards off the beach, the massive Federal warship was slowly pounding Battery Wagner into submission. Worst of all, Stoney saw that the heaviest projectiles fired by the Confederate guns failed to penetrate her armored sides.

The sight fascinated him. Eleven other ships were participating in the bombardment—six turreted ships of the monitor type and five wooden vessels. Compared to the *New Ironsides*, however, their effect was meager.

The sight that chilled Theodore Stoney's heart—the *New Ironsides* and two monitors firing on Confederate fortifications.

Illustrated London News

The wooden ships could be disregarded; their days were over. The new turreted monitors carried too few guns and their fire was too slow for successful offensive operations. But the *New Ironsides*, Stoney realized with a chill in his heart, was another story.

As a matter of fact she was the most formidable vessel built by the Federal government during the War Between the States. An immense armored steamship carrying fourteen 11-inch guns and one 8-inch rifle, she was the first American battleship in the real sense of the term. Union Admiral Louis M. Goldsborough declared her to be "a much more efficient type of ironclad than the monitors," and Admiral Dahlgren described her as "a fine powerful ship." Though three or four British and French vessels of the era exceeded her in tonnage, none of these ever proved themselves in battle, while the *New Ironsides* was more often in action and was hit by return fire more frequently than any other vessel in existence. Undoubtedly, in the summer of 1863, the *New Ironsides* was one of the most powerful warships in the world—perhaps the most powerful.

The USS *New Ironsides* as she appeared off Charleston
Official Records Navy

As Stoney watched her hammer Battery Wagner into rubble, he realized that she might be the gravest menace yet confronting the Confederacy. Already she had practically silenced the guns of the battery. Given time, he believed, she could demolish Fort Sumter, destroy or capture Charleston, and then move against the few remaining ports of the blockaded South with what foreboding results no one could tell.

She must not be given that time. She had to be stopped—but how?

* * * * *

In July, prior to Carlin's aborted attack with the *Torch*, Captain Lee had written to Captain Armand Beauregard, the general's brother and an aide on his staff.

I would further state that the small torpedo steamer (Winan's model) now building on the Cooper River, is nearly complete, and we have good reason to expect will aid materially in the defense of this city.[1]

The "small torpedo steamer" alluded to by Lee was the first vessel designed exclusively from the keel up as a torpedo boat. Even though the Special Service Detachment with their rowboats, and later Lee's torpedo ram, the *Torch*, had failed to sink an enemy warship, they nevertheless had proven that the spar-mounted torpedo was a feasible weapon. In addition, particularly after the attempt on the *New Ironsides* by the *Torch*, Union commanders became extremely anxious over such attacks and ordered that numerous precautionary measures be taken. With the advent of the small fast torpedo steamers, Federal commanders would have even more cause to worry.

After observing the devastating fire from the *New Ironsides*, Stoney sought out his longtime friend and business partner, Dr. St. Julien Ravenel, who was serving at the military hospital in Columbia, South Carolina. Ravenel and Stoney jointly managed the Southern Torpedo Company of Charleston which manufactured explosive devices including some of Captain Lee's torpedoes. Fortunately, Ravenel, was on furlough and at his home on the Battery at Charleston, and the two men discussed the peril that was lurking just off shore. Stoney was adamant—unless they could find some means of destroying the *New Ironsides*, the war would be lost. Ravenel reportedly produced a scale model of a craft which had been constructed by Ross Winan, an ardent Southern sympathizer from Baltimore. A small boat such as this might carry one of Captain Lee's torpedoes to the very side of the Union warship. Stoney's excitement grew. He would pay $25,000 toward the construction costs if Ravenel could build such a boat.

A few days later, Ravenel sent word to Stoney that he had formulated a plan. Ravenel owned a plantation called Stoney Landing approximately 30 miles up the Cooper River northeast of Charleston. In addition to the usual plantation fare of crops and livestock, the doctor had been experimenting with the making of lime from the outcroppings of marl along the bluffs above the river. In addition, since the beginning of the war, he had set up a niter (used in the making of gunpowder) works on behalf of the Confederate government. Here, away from the prying eyes of Federal spies, he could build a boat that, he believed, could destroy the *New Ironsides*.

Stoney, too, had encouraging news. Other Charleston entrepreneurs, including Theodore Wagner and Chap Chevis, had come forward and offered to help finance the project. With financial backing secured, Ravenel's next step was to see David C. Ebaugh who was superintendent of the niter works at his plantation on the Cooper River.

Upon his arrival, Ravenel asked Ebaugh if he thought he could build a small boat with a long pole attached to the stem that could carry one of Captain Lee's torpedoes. Because of the smallness of the vessel, Ravenel suggested that it be man-powered. Ebaugh, an expert machinist, objected to the idea that the boat be powered by hand saying that it would require too many crew members and would be too slow. Instead, he proposed building a cigar-shaped vessel and installing a small steam engine to power it. Ravenel was skeptical that an engine small enough to fit in the boat could be found, and even if such an engine existed, would be too noisy. Ebaugh knew of a small double engine, he said, that had been used to drive the machinery at the Northeastern Railroad Shop. The engine had been replaced by a larger one and now lay idle. With slight modifications, and by muffling the exhaust, he was confident he could make it work in the torpedo boat. After listening to the machinist's arguments, Ravenel was convinced and instructed Ebaugh to begin construction immediately.

Ebaugh wasted little time. The engine was acquired and John Chaulk, master of machinery at the Northeastern Railroad, agreed to be responsible for its installation. All manual labor and carpentry work was performed by Ravenel's Negro plantation workers. In a postwar letter, Ebaugh provided the only known account of the construction details of the vessel that would later be christened the CSS *David*:

> I laid out the boat full size under a niter shed at Stoney Landing. It was 5 feet in diameter and 48½ feet long, 18 feet of the middle of the boat was the same size tapering to a point at each end. The ends were made of large pine logs turned off with a grove to receive the ends of the planking, the timbers were made of 1½ inch oak doubled and riveted together, they were placed about 15 inches apart, the planking was the whole length 1½ inches thick hollowed on the inside to fit the timbers and rounded on outside, the planking was riveted to the timbers, the whole was put together at Stoney Landing, chalked and launched. It was sent to Charleston to have the machinery put in. It was there hoisted out of the water by a crane on the Northeastern Railroad wharf, put on a car and carried to the railroad shop.[2]

The *David* was like nothing ever seen before. Her cylindrical hull, which was painted a light blue, was heavily ballasted and allowed only about half of her convex deck to remain above the water. Ravenel experienced the same frustration as Lee when it came time to install her iron covering—there was none available. The armor would have to come later. Most reports indicate that ballast tanks were incorporated into the fore and aft sections of the hull, that when filled caused her to float even lower in the water leaving only the smokestack and the coaming around her crew position visible above the surface. While most David's are thought to have had these tanks, it is possible that the original *David* did not, for Ebaugh described what amounted to diving planes in the same manner as the submarine *Hunley*. After the war he wrote that he had provided "bars of iron extending on both sides of the boat hung on trunnions so as to raise it out of the water when the boat was in motion and let it down when near the object."[3]

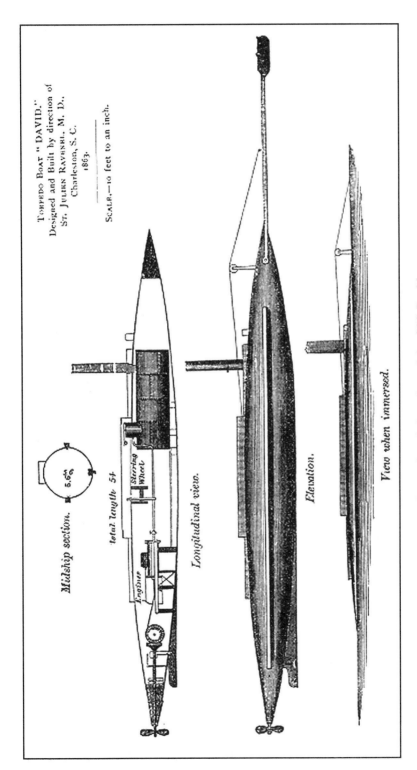

Internal and plan view of the CSS *David*

The small boiler, which Ebaugh claimed was spirited out of Fort Sumter in the dead of night, was placed forward, the engine aft. In between, in what was called a "cuddyhole," was a station for the helmsman. Later, lines and a windless were added which enabled the raising and lowering of the torpedo spar from inside the cuddyhole. Also later, iron would become available and a thin covering of ¼-inch steel plate would be attached to her upper surface and the smokestack. A two-bladed propeller drove her forward, and subsequent tests would indicate that she could do over 10 knots, considerably more than the projected six or seven.

After the installation of her machinery at the railroad shop, the *David* was hauled to the Cooper River where she was launched at the Atlantic Wharf situated at the east end of Broad Street. It was at this time, at the suggestion of Dr. Ravenel's wife, that the vessel was officially named *David*, although David Ebaugh insisted in later years that the boat was named after him. Much to the relief of her builders, she floated as designed. The Confederate Navy took charge of the boat, and Captain Lee wasted little time in affixing a 14-foot piece of three-inch boiler tube to her pointed stem. One of his deadly torpedoes, containing 70 pounds of fine rifle powder, was secured to the other end. This spar torpedo projected ahead of the boat six or seven feet below the surface and initially was fixed in place before leaving the dock.[4]

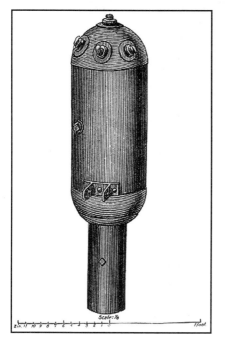

Drawing of a copper spar torpedo which appears in the Navy *Official Records*

Official Records Navy

Shortly after the launching, Lieutenant Glassell and his men arrived in Charleston from Wilmington where they had been manning the ironclad CSS *North Carolina*. Confederate authorities, anticipating an imminent Federal attack on the outer defenses, had hastily transferred Glassell and his men to the South Carolina city. The Wilmington men were distributed among the various ships of the Charleston Squadron as reinforcements, and Glassell, who was not needed on the ironclads, was left with no immediate duty to perform.

Theodore Stoney invited Glassell to inspect the *David*, and with Flag Officer Tucker's approval, offered him her command if he thought he could utilize the torpedo boat to attack the enemy. Glassell eagerly accepted and wrote:

On examination I determined to make a trial. She was yet in an un-finished state. Assistant Engineer J. H. Tomb (James H.) volunteered his services, and all the necessary machinery was soon fitted and got in working order. James Stuart (alias Sullivan) volunteered to go as fireman, and afterwards the services of J. W. Cannon (J. Walker) as pilot was secured. The boat was ballasted so as to float deeply in the water, and all above painted the most invisible color. I had also an armament on deck (in addition to the torpedo) of four double-barrel shot guns, and as many navy revolvers; also, four cork life preservers had been thrown on board, and made us feel safe.[5]

Engineer Tomb had seen his share of war up to this point. Born in Savannah, Georgia, he had declined an appointment as a third assistant engineer in U.S. service after which he resigned and offered his services to the Confederacy. He had served on the CSS *Jackson* and CSS *McRae* during the Battle of New Orleans in April of 1862, where he was taken prisoner and sent north to Fort Warren. Exchanged on August 5, he was currently serving as an engineer on board the CSS *Chicora* of the Charleston Squadron. Tomb had been on board that ironclad when she, in concert with the *Palmetto State*, attacked the Federal blockading fleet off Charleston in January of 1863. The helmsman, J. Walker Cannon, came from the *Palmetto State*, and fireman James Stuart, who is referred to as "alias Sullivan," may have been a Northerner with Southern sympathies.

Lieutenant Glassell began an intense training period during which he found that the *David* handled well and was reasonably speedy under a full head of steam. After performing several practice attacks on some of the Confederate ironclads in Charleston harbor, Glassell felt he was ready and applied for authorization from Flag Officer Tucker to attack one of the Union warships. The Confederate commander gave his consent, and Glassell began final preparations for a sortie that night. Later he wrote of his experience:

> The 5th of October, 1863, a little after dark, we left Charleston and proceeded with the ebb tide down the harbor. A light north wind was blowing, and the night was slightly hazy, but starlight, and the water was smooth. I desired to make the attack about the turn of the tide, and this ought to have been just after nine o'clock, but the north wind made it run out a little longer.
>
> We passed Fort Sumter and beyond the line of picket-boats without being discovered. Silently steaming along just inside the bar, I had a good opportunity to reconnoiter the whole fleet of the enemy at anchor between me and the campfires on Morris Island....Quietly maneuvering and observing the enemy, I was half an hour or more waiting on time and tide. The music of drum and fife had just ceased, and the nine o'clock gun had been fired from the admiral's ship, as a signal for all unnecessary

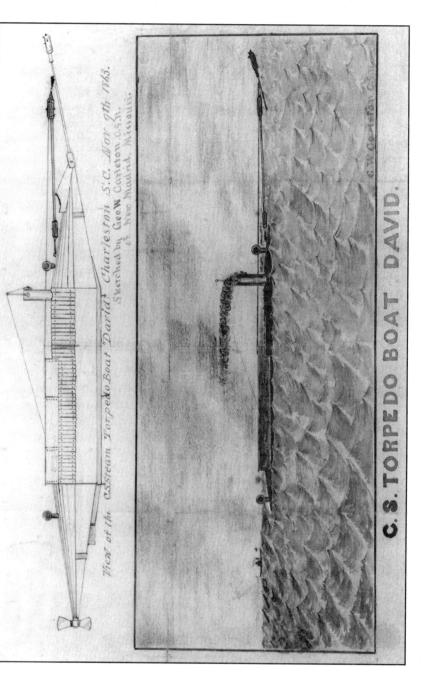

View of the C.S. Steam Torpedo Boat "David" Charleston S:C. Nov 9th 1863.
Sketched by Geo W. Carleton, C.S.N.
of New Madrid. Missouri.

C. S. TORPEDO BOAT DAVID.

G. W. Carleton C.S.

An extremely accurate sketch of the *David* rendered by Paymaster George W. Carleton, CSN. The drawing shows to good effect the apparatus for the raising and lowering of the torpedo.

lights to be extinguished and for the men not on watch to retire for sleep. I thought the proper time for attack had arrived.[6]

Glassell turned the *David* toward the looming black shape in the distance, which was the *New Ironsides*. Off to his left (he was approaching from seaward), the distant campfires of the Union soldiers on Morris Island were barely discernible through the haze. Federal sailors recently captured by the Confederates had indicated that the fleet was on guard for an expected torpedo attack. Because of this, Glassell anticipated that they would be discovered, and that there would be heavy fire directed toward the *David*.

My guns were loaded with buckshot. I knew that if the officer of the deck could be disabled to begin with, it would cause them some confusion and increase our chances for escape, so I determined that if the occasion offered, I would commence by firing the first shot. Accordingly, having on a full head of steam, I took charge of the helm, it being so arranged that I could sit on deck and work the wheel with my feet. Then directing the engineer and fireman to keep below and give me all possible speed, I gave a double-barrel gun to the pilot with instructions not to fire until I should do so, and steered directly for the monitor [*New Ironsides*]. I intended to strike her just under the gang-way, but the tide still running out, carried us to a point neared the quarter. Thus we rapidly approached the enemy.[7]

The old locomotive engine was pounding for all it was worth. Squeezed behind the roaring boiler, Sullivan struggled to get one more shovel of coal on the blazing fire, while aft, Tomb checked the gauges and banged the throttle wide open. Cannon, relieved now of piloting duties, crouched behind the coaming of the cuddyhole trying to keep his shotgun leveled on the target, while Glassell, steering with his feet, concentrated on keeping the torpedo boat on course. With a dry mouth and pounding heart, Glassell drove the onrushing *David* straight for the massive Federal warship.

When within about 300 yards of her, a sentinel hailed us: "Boat ahoy! Boat ahoy!" repeating the hail several times very rapidly. We were coming towards them with all speed, and I made no answer, but cocked both barrels of my gun. The officer of the deck [Ensign Charles W. Howard] now made his appearance, and loudly demanded, "What boat is that?" Being now within forty yards of the ship, and with plenty of headway to carry us on, I thought it about time the fight should commence, and I fired my gun. [Glassell fired both barrels of his shotgun.] The officer of the deck fell back mortally wounded (poor fellow), and I ordered the engine stopped. The next moment the torpedo struck the vessel and exploded.[8]

A tremendous blast rocked both the *New Ironsides* and the diminutive *David*. The huge warship shuddered from the blow and heeled violently to port. Rigging came crashing to the deck. Guns were thrown from their mounts, and shot and shell spun dizzily across her decks. The *David*, too, was badly shaken. A giant geyser of water rose one hundred feet in the air and came down with a resounding crash upon the torpedo boat. The cuddyhole was swamped; water cascading down the funnel extinguished the fire in the furnace. Rifle and pistol shots splattered against the *David* as a half-dazed Glassell shouted for Tomb to reverse the engine and back off. Tomb shouted back that the collision had loosened some of the ballast which had jammed the machinery. The engine could not be moved. While her four crew members crouched in the flooded cuddyhole, a shower of bullets slammed into the torpedo boat as it drifted helplessly past the shaken *New Ironsides*. Glassell gave the order to abandon ship.

Taking one of the cork life preservers, he dived into the water and began swimming away. Cannon, a non-swimmer, slipped over the unexposed side of the *David* and hung on to her for dear life, while Federal sailors and marines poured a heavy fire into the helpless boat. The Federals were aided in their aim by a "bull's-eye" lantern which somehow had not been extinguished and was still burning in the cuddyhole. Heavy guns began to thunder, sending grape and canister whistling over the struggling Confederates. Engineer Tomb dived overboard, and like Glassell, swam with all his strength to escape the hissing missiles. Sullivan, however, caught hold of one of the *New Ironside's* rudder-chains as the damaged *David* drifted by, where he would cling for hours before being discovered and taken prisoner.[9]

The *David* strikes the *New Ironsides*.

Naval Historical Center

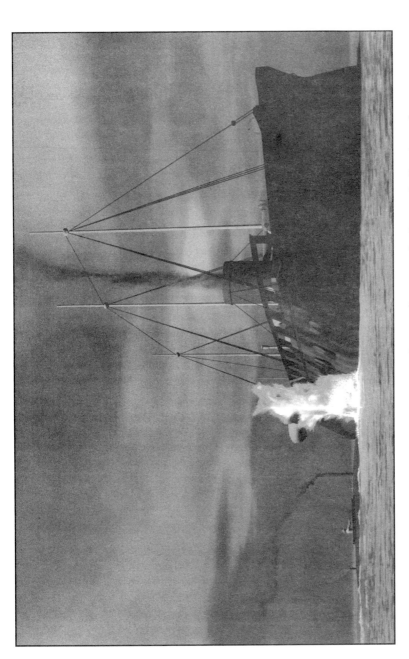

The *David* is swamped by the deluge of water thrown up by her exploding torpedo.

Courtesy of Dan Dowdey

"I swam some distance down the harbor," Tomb wrote afterward, "but finding that my clothing was impeding my progress, and looking back and seeing that the *David* was still afloat, I concluded to return and try to save her." The torpedo boat had by this time drifted off into the darkness and the firing had slackened. Tomb, exhausted and cold, reached her side and dragged himself aboard. To his surprise he found the shivering Cannon still clinging to the coaming of the cuddyhole. Quickly, he helped the pilot aboard, and together they began to move the ballast that had jammed the machinery. Soon the shafts and gears were free, but there was little steam left in the boiler. Taking fire from the still-burning lantern, Tomb relit the furnace, and soon the steam gauge showed a rise in pressure.

In a few minutes there was enough pressure to start the engine, and when Tomb opened the valves, the *David* moved slowly off into the night. He later wrote:

> We proceeded up the harbor, turning between the *Ironsides* and a monitor to prevent them from using their heavy guns on us in passing. The *Ironsides* fired three shots from her heavy guns which passed over us. All this time there was a heavy fire directed on the *David* from small arms from the deck of the *Ironsides*, riddling every part of the *David* above water. As we returned up the harbor we passed through the fleet and by the guard boats without further damage to us, and rounding under the stern of the flagship, I made my report to Flag Officer Tucker with nothing on but my undershirt.[10]

Meanwhile, Lieutenant Glassell was still struggling in the water.

> The enemy in no amiable mood poured down upon the bubbling water a hailstorm of rifle and pistol shots from the deck of the *Ironsides*, and from the nearest monitor. Sometimes they struck very close to my head, but swimming for my life, I soon disappeared from their sight, and found myself all alone in the water. I hoped that with the assistance of the flood-tide, I might be able to reach Fort Sumter, but a north wind was against me, and after I had been in the water more than an hour, I became numb with cold, and was nearly exhausted. Just then the boat of a transport schooner picked me up, and found, to their surprise, that they had captured a rebel.[11]

The attack had taken the Federal vessel almost completely by surprise. The night was very dark and hazy, and the *David* was not seen by those on board the *New Ironsides* until the torpedo boat was almost upon them. In his official report, Commodore Stephen C. Rowan, commander of the Union warship, described what was seen from the deck of the *Ironsides* in those final minutes:

> About a minute before the explosion a small object was seen by the sentinels and hailed by them as a boat, and also by Mr. Howard, officer of the deck, from the gangway. Receiving no answer, he gave the order

"fire into her." The sentinels delivered their fire, and immediately the ship received a very severe blow from the explosion, throwing a column of water upon the spar deck and into the engine room. The object fired at proved to be (as I subsequently learned from one of the prisoners) a torpedo steamer, shaped like a cigar, 50 feet long by 5 feet in diameter, and of great speed, and so submerged that the only portion of her visible was the coamings of her hatch, which were only 2 feet above the water's edge and about 10 feet in length.[12]

The following morning, Confederate authorities were dismayed to see the *New Ironsides* still swinging lazily at her anchor. From shore there appeared to be no apparent damage. Federal divers examined the hull in the vicinity of the explosion and reported that, aside from a slight dent, the only visible damage was some missing copper. Their reports, however, would prove to be woefully inadequate.

By sheer chance, and unknown to the Confederates at the time, the torpedo had exploded where a structural bulkhead abutted the hull and the bulkhead absorbed most of the concussion. Beauregard believed that the charge of 70 pounds was too small; however, Glassell felt, as did many others including Captain Lee, that even the 70-pound torpedo, if exploded a foot or two lower against the hull, would have certainly sent the giant warship to the bottom.

The *New Ironsides* remained at her anchorage off Morris Island and as coal was consumed from her bunkers adjacent to the bulkhead, much more serious damage became apparent. In November, the ship's carpenter carefully inspected the inside of the hull and found the vessel very seriously damaged. He reported that a large support beam was badly split, the framing of the engine room had a crack four feet in length, stanchions and numerous lap knees were torn from their mounts, and the ceiling of the coal bunkers had been forced inward approximately 10 inches. "In my opinion," he wrote, "this ship ought to be docked as soon as she can possibly be spared from this harbor."[13]

Towed to the Federal base at Port Royal, South Carolina, repairs were attempted, but a dry dock was needed so she was towed north to the Philadelphia Navy Yard. During repairs at Philadelphia, it was discovered, in addition to the carpenter's findings, that her hull and supports had been severely weakened, a large deck beam had been driven "on end," and several knees abutting the hull had been shattered. The severe damage was kept a secret for the remainder of the war so that the Confederates would never learn just how close they had come to destroying the largest warship in the Federal Navy. The *New Ironsides* was kept out of action for over a year, and after returning to duty off Wilmington, North Carolina, never lobbed her massive shells into Charleston again.[14]

Lieutenant Glassell was imprisoned at Fort Lafayette and later at Fort Warren in Boston harbor for more than a year. Rear Admiral John A.

Dahlgren, Federal commander of the Union blockading squadron on the South Atlantic coast, did not want to see Glassell exchanged. In a letter to Secretary Welles on October 12, he stated: "It is desirable that this officer should not be allowed to return here until some time has elapsed, as he could not fail to be of great service to the enemy in future operations of the same kind."[15]

During Glassell's imprisonment at Fort Warren, he received word that the Confederate Congress had promoted him to commander, "for gallant and meritorious conduct in attempting the destruction of the U.S. ironclad frigate *New Ironsides* by torpedo in Charleston Harbor on the night of 5th October, 1863, and to rank from that date." Finally exchanged on October 18, 1864, Glassell was given command of the ironclad *Fredericksburg* of the James River Squadron. Upon the evacuation of Richmond six months later, he was attached to the Semmes Naval Brigade and was later paroled at Greensboro, North Carolina, on April 28, 1865.[16]

Tomb was also promoted to chief engineer and given command of the *David*. The torpedo boat was repaired and the mechanism for raising and lowering the spar from the cuddyhole was installed. A quarter-inch layer of steel was attached to her upper sides to deflect small arms fire, and a cap was fabricated over the stack to prevent water from entering after an explosion.

The attacks by the *Torch* and the *David* demonstrated the capability and the outright audacity of the Confederates at Charleston, and the repercussions were not lost on an apprehensive Federal fleet. The men of the Southern Navy had come very close to destroying the largest warship in the Union inventory, and as a result, Admiral Dahlgren ordered every monitor to take extra precautions that, hopefully, would forestall any future attacks. Each monitor was instructed to anchor at a predetermined position, extra lookouts were posted, and immense log booms were placed around each vessel. Cutters with armed sailors and marines patrolled the areas between the monitors at night, while calcium searchlights constantly pierced the darkness looking for any sign of a torpedo boat. During the day the Union warships controlled the outer harbor and the area offshore, but at night the Confederates ruled these waters, allowing for the transportation of supplies and reinforcements to the outlying fortifications and providing sanctuary for an occasional blockade runner.

On October 7, 1863, just two days after the attack by the *David*, Admiral Dahlgren in a confidential report to the Navy Department at Washington summed it up best:

> Among the many inventions with which I have been familiar, I have seen none which have acted so perfectly at first trial. The secrecy, rapidity of movement, control of direction, and precise explosion indicate, I think, the introduction of the torpedo element as a means of certain warfare. It can be ignored no longer. If 60 pounds of powder, why not 600 pounds?[17]

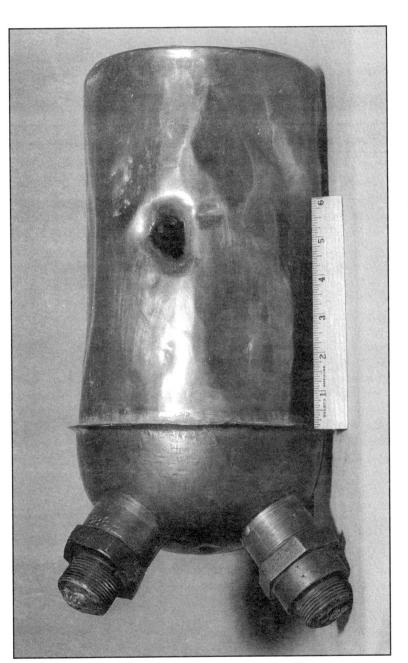

A surviving example of a Confederate spar torpedo
West Point Museum Collections, U.S. Military Academy

CHAPTER 6

THE "DAVID" CLASS TORPEDO BOATS

For the most part, Confederate torpedo boats fall into one of two categories—the David class and the Squib class. The David class refers to any "cigar"-shaped, steam-driven type vessel designed specifically to deliver an explosive charge to the side of an enemy ship. These boats had enclosed hulls and ballast tanks which enabled them to partially submerge and assume a very low profile in the water. The class takes its name from the original *David* designed by Dr. St. Julien Ravenel and assisted by Captain Francis D. Lee. The Squib class includes all vessels similar to the CSS *Squib* and consists of those steam-driven boats which were designed and constructed as open launches with a torpedo spar on the bow. The Squib class will be covered in a subsequent chapter. Obviously the *Torch* and the torpedo rowboats do not fit into either of these two categories and were, therefore, considered in prior chapters of this book.

Unfortunately, the exact number of David-type torpedo boats built by the Confederacy is unknown. Most, if not all, detailed records concerning their construction and operations were destroyed at the end of the war to prevent any possible Federal reprisals against those who employed "an engine of destruction not recognized by the rules of war." From documentation contained in both the Navy and Army *Official Records*, along with private correspondence, it is known that additional Davids were built at Charleston and at Stoney Landing on the Cooper River, construction site of the original *David*. Besides Charleston, torpedo boats were also built at such places as: Mobile and Selma, Alabama; Savannah and Columbus, Georgia; Peedee River Bridge, South Carolina; Shreveport, Louisiana; Richmond, Virginia; Wilmington, North Carolina; and overseas in England. All of these, with the exception of one at Mobile, those at Charleston, and possibly one at Wilmington, appear to fall into the Squib class.

Even before Glassell's attack on the *New Ironsides*, David Ebaugh had begun construction of another David at his landing on the Cooper River. With the partial success of the attack, other Davids were laid down at various locations in and around the city. It would take time, however, for these to reach operational status given the shortage of materials and skilled labor that always plagued ship construction in the South during the war. When Engineer Tomb rounded to beside the *Palmetto State* that night with nothing on but his undershirt, he was not about to stay idle for long. Reports of encounters with torpedo boats by Union sailors in subsequent nights are too numerous to be written off as just the imagination of a nervous and jittery Federal fleet.

On the night of October 7, just two days after the *New Ironsides* was rocked by the explosion of *David's* torpedo, Master Alvin Phinney, commander of the U.S. Mortar Schooner *Racer*, sent Acting Master's Mate D. B. Corey to patrol off Fort Sumter.

> Last evening at 6 o'clock I sent a boat in charge of D. B. Corey, acting master's mate, on picket up in the vicinity of Fort Sumter. Mr. Corey reports that he saw nothing until about 9:30, when he heard one of the monitors firing musketry. [He] pulled up to her, and was told there was some kind of a craft going toward the fleet. [He] pulled after her, and saw what appeared to be a large boat, but could not see any oars. [He] pulled back to the *Catskill* and reported it, when he was ordered down to the *Ironsides* [where he] reported to her, and was ordered to pull out on the bar in about 2 fathoms, and lay around there, which he did until 4 o'clock this morning, when he returned on board, it being then quite light.[1]

The fact that one of the monitors saw and fired at the torpedo boat, and Corey gave chase to a large boat with no oars, lends credence to Phinney's report. Because records indicate that no blockade runners arrived at or cleared from Charleston on this night, and many Federals saw the boat and some fired at it, we would have to conclude that it was Tomb and the *David*. This sortie by the *David* proved unsuccessful, but Tomb was back two nights later. Master Phinney later reported that, by now, a very tense Master's Mate Corey had the dubious distinction of again giving chase:

> Last evening at 7 o'clock I sent a boat in charge of Acting Master's Mate D. B. Corey on picket. Mr. Corey reports that he saw nothing until about 11, when he saw something which appeared to be about 10 feet long above water, going very fast. It appeared to extend some ways under water by the ripple it made both ahead and astern. It soon passed out of sight, and he saw nothing more. He returned on board at 4:15 this a.m.[2]

The sightings of something "10 feet long above water," and "going very fast" are significant in that the dimensions of the "cuddyhole" closely match the Union officer's description, and the *David* was considered fast at full throttle. Corey's observation that much of the vessel was submerged also indicates that this was indeed the *David*.

Chief Engineer James H. Tomb, CSN
Southern Historical Collection, University of North Carolina

Tomb and the *David* were evidently very active this night, for a bit later the U.S. Schooner *Dan Smith* had a frightening brush with the torpedo boat as reported by the schooner's commander, Acting Master Benjamin C. Dean:

At 10:15 p.m. of the 9th instant the sentry discovered the torpedo boat. When about 80 yards distant, the hail not being answered, I ordered the men to fire. I immediately called all hands to quarters. They appeared to be trying to cross my vessel's bow, but, being fired on, they backed off and headed to the southward until after passing my vessel. The boat moves rapidly and with very little noise. I discharged about sixty rounds of musketry at them as they passed my vessel with what effect I am unable to say.[3]

On October 17, 1863, Admiral Dahlgren from the flagship USS *Philadelphia* reported to Secretary Welles that: "Last night an object, believed to be a torpedo boat, was seen by our picket boat and one or two of the vessels. On finding itself discovered, it returned up the harbor."[4]

The Federal ironclad monitor USS *Catskill* was at her station off Sullivan's Island during this time. From that position her commander, Greenleaf Cilley, had observed large numbers of laborers who were busy strengthening the fortifications at Battery Marshal and had also noted a large number of Confederate troops moving toward Breach Inlet at the north end of the island. In the early morning hours of October 20, however, he saw something that must have sent shivers down his spine:

About 3:00 this morning our lookouts hailed a low, dark object approaching us on our starboard quarter, nearly astern. No reply being

Painting by an unknown artist of a David class torpedo boat being prepared for a nightly sortie

Naval Historical Center

given to the hails, [we] opened fire with rifles. It kept away, and shortly after approached on the port quarter, nearly aft. Fired again at it, and it kept away toward the *Ironsides*. Made signal 597, got underway, and steamed to near the *Ironsides* and back to our station without seeing more of the object. It approached us so near aft that we could not bring our turret guns to bear upon it.[5]

Captain Lee had not been idle during this time. On October 15, he had written to A. N. Toutant Beauregard, the commanding officer's brother, proposing that he be authorized to continue with the construction of additional Davids.

> Accompanying this note please find a hasty sketch of my device of cigar steamer for carrying spar torpedoes, which you would oblige me by submitting to the inspection of the general commanding. In several respects it varies from the original device, and I believe is far more effective. I have increased the size of the torpedo, and have given it greater submersion.
>
> That a fleet of these little steamers is capable of destroying the enemy's ironclads is not only my opinion, but the conviction of every naval officer with whom I have conversed. Commodore Tucker has informed me that the greatest eagerness to volunteer for this service has been expressed by the officers and men of his command.
>
> I hope, if the Government will not act promptly, that I may be allowed to devote a portion of my attention to the carrying out of several private projects which have been proposed.[6]

Beauregard approved Lee's request and even offered to allow him to continue to work with the Southern Torpedo Company in the building of additional boats. The commanding general was still enthusiastic about the potential of torpedo boats and in an endorsement to Lee's request stated that he "would like very much to have one dozen at least of these boats for the defense of the coast of this department."[7] Beauregard, however, still bemoaned the fact that the government in Richmond was not forthcoming with material and personnel to aid in the boats' construction.

Captain Lee was proud of his work and resented any attempts by others of copying his inventions without his supervision. A certain Captain John Ferguson had evidently applied to other parties for the production of torpedoes which utilized fuses different from those designed by Lee, and which were intended for use on "cigar steamers." On October 24, 1863, Lee wrote to Ferguson objecting to the captain's actions. The first paragraph of this letter is enlightening in that it very accurately describes Lee's development of the spar torpedo and the boat to deliver it:

> I have for the last two years been perfecting a new mode of naval attack, on which I had hoped to make a reputation as a military engineer. The great object I had in view in developing my plans was to defeat

the enormous naval power of the enemy by a simple, cheap, and readily accomplished device. I first demonstrated, and afterward proved by actual experiment, that torpedoes borne at the extremities of spars may be exploded against the vessels of the enemy with little danger to the boats carrying them. I have designed a variety of vessels adapted for this especial purpose, and have fallen on the cigar form as one giving greatest speed, and offering the least vulnerable surface above the water line. I have also devised a variety of torpedoes, and arranged various modes for firing them. Out of all of them I have selected the one now in general use by our gunboats as best offering the advantages sought, viz, certainty of fire, security against moisture, and safety in handling. This latter requisite I have laid great stress upon, inasmuch as the torpedoes had frequently to be placed in the hands of parties who would not exercise those proper cautions which a more delicate arrangement may require.[8]

Meanwhile Beauregard decided to make one more attempt to move the Richmond government to action, this time in the expectation of deploying a whole fleet of torpedo boats. On November 14, 1863, the commanding general sent Congressman Miles a lengthy letter outlining, in Beauregard's estimation, six major reasons why the ironclads of the Charleston Squadron were totally useless. These included their slow speed and deep draft, their inability to survive shots from the enemy's 15-inch guns while their own guns were hampered by overly small gun ports which limited their range. In addition, Beauregard criticized the Confederate ironclads for their inability to survive in the open ocean, their poor living conditions, and the tremendous cost they had accrued to the country in labor and materials.

Instead of pouring material and labor into vessels such as these, the general proposed a whole fleet of steam-driven torpedo boats:

> The enemy's iron-clads being invulnerable to shots above water beyond 800 yards, they should be attacked below water. The best way to accomplish this is by means of swift sea-going steamers, capable of traveling 10 or 12 miles an hour, shot-proof above water and armed with Capt. F. D. Lee's submarine repeating spar torpedo, which is both simple and certain in its operation. Not one of his submarine torpedoes has yet failed to explode on striking a resisting object. The experiment of the *David*, a small cigar torpedo-boat, against the *New Ironsides*, shows the effect of a 70-pound torpedo, only 6 feet below water, on the thick sides— over 5 feet—of that sea monster. Since the attack, about one month ago, the *New Ironsides* has not fired one shot, notwithstanding the renewed bombardment of Sumter has been going on twenty days and nights, showing evidently that she has been seriously injured.[9]

Beauregard warmed to his argument and went on to state that he firmly believed that with one-half dozen of these boats the blockade of the

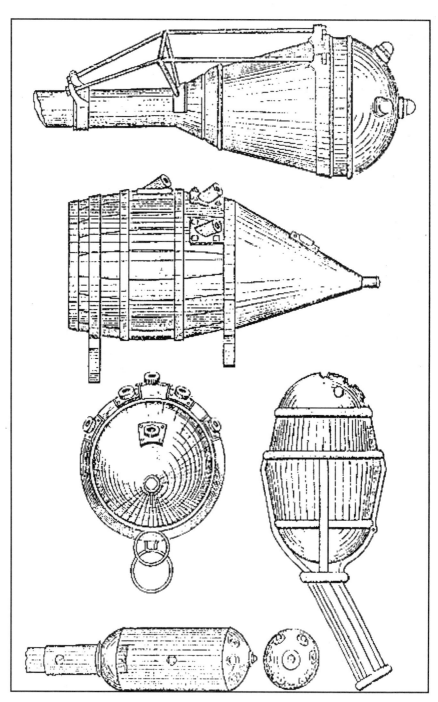

Several examples of spar torpedoes. The larger ones were typically mounted on heavier vessels such as the ironclads *Chicora* and *Palmetto State*. The small torpedo at the bottom was utilized by torpedo boats.

Barnes: *Submarine Warfare*, 1869

Atlantic and Gulf coasts could be raised and the Federals driven out of the Mississippi River. While it is arguable that the commanding general's vision of the war was confined to his own department, his final statement is significantly profound when viewed from more than a century later:

> Indeed, a few years hence, we will ask ourselves in astonishment, how it was that with such a great discovery, offering such magnificent results, we never applied it to any useful purpose in this contest for our homes and independence.[10]

It was Beauregard's intent that Congressman Miles present his arguments on the floor of the House, but instead Miles took the letter to Secretary of the Navy Mallory. The naval secretary politely agreed with the general on several points, but in a lengthy reply to Miles pointed out that the Confederate ironclads were designed for harbor defense and for that purpose they were eminently suited. The Confederate Navy in home waters was committed to fighting in the harbors and rivers of the South, not on the open sea.

With obviously more wisdom and judgment than the general had displayed, Mallory tactfully pointed out that the torpedo boat was not the only answer. It was quite easy, as the Federals at Charleston were in the process of doing, to surround warships with protective nettings of chains and logs making them practically invulnerable to torpedo attack. There was a possibility, as Beauregard had suggested, that larger boats could be built in England and Mallory promised he would try, but because of the neutrality laws he was not very hopeful. Although conceding that the torpedo boat held great possibilities, the naval secretary felt that they had yet to prove themselves as a viable weapon, and respectfully returned Beauregard's letter to Congressman Miles. There would be no help in the foreseeable future from the Navy Department.[11]

Beauregard next turned to the army engineers and convinced them to build a couple of Davids. Lee was put in charge, and on December 20, wrote a letter to Colonel D. B. Harris, chief engineer of the department, requesting that the Henery Machine Shop be turned over to him solely for the fabrication of engines for the torpedo boats. Mr. W. S. Henery, with whom Lee had previously worked, had shown the captain his drawings for "double engines" which Lee believed would fit perfectly into the small confines of the Davids. Lee requested that the department stop Henery's work on anchors, artillery shells, and gun carriages, and order him to devote his shop exclusively to the manufacturing of these engines. After numerous written exchanges in which Major N. R. Chambliss, commander of the Charleston Arsenal, complained bitterly that he could not afford to lose one of his best machine shops, Beauregard acquiesced and informed Lee that he would have to look elsewhere for the engines.

In spite of these difficulties, additional boats were being built. In January of 1864, Lee wrote to Lieutenant Colonel A. L. Rives, acting chief of the

Engineering Bureau in Richmond, requesting that certain supplies be forwarded to Charleston, and proposing that a special corps be instituted for men in the torpedo service. Lee further suggested that Congress grant "a large percentage" of the value of any Federal vessel captured or destroyed to the members of this corps, and that local shipyards be authorized to make direct purchases of building materials as they saw fit. Rives replied that in order to aid this enterprise, Lee was authorized to export cotton to Nassau in exchange for badly needed hardware. In addition, Rives reported that steps had been taken at Mobile to begin construction of Davids just as soon as Lee would send the necessary plans.[12]

As construction progressed on additional boats at Charleston, Engineer Tomb and the original *David* were about to become involved in a most secret operation. On August 12, 1863, a strange-looking craft had been unloaded from two flatcars and launched at a small dock at the end of Calhoun Street. The vessel causing so much excitement among observers was a submersible, which had been built at Mobile, Alabama, and shipped to Charleston by rail. Later the submarine, which was often referred to as a "torpedo boat," would be christened the CSS *H. L. Hunley* and would become famous as the first successful submarine to sink an enemy ship. The *Hunley*, which towed its torpedo astern on a long line and was hand powered, was by the end of 1863, attempting to attack the Federal monitors lying offshore. The intent was to approach an enemy ironclad on a moonless night, dive beneath the vessel and surface on the other side while pulling the torpedo against the ship where it would explode. Her commander, army Lieutenant George E. Dixon, however, found that it was extremely taxing on the crew to crank the submarine all the way from the Mount Pleasant dock to several miles out to sea in order to reach the enemy ironclads offshore.

After returning from an especially weary and unsuccessful patrol in early December, Dixon determined that the only way to husband the strength of his crew was on future missions to arrange for the submarine while on the surface to be towed to the outer harbor. Reporting his idea to General Beauregard, the commanding general advised him to seek out Engineer Tomb and the *David*.

Flag Officer John R. Tucker, commanding the Charleston Squadron, ordered Tomb to assist the *Hunley* and soon towing operations began. Tomb would tow the submarine, weather permitting, one to two miles out to sea where the towline would be cast off, and the *David* would proceed on her own sortie or return to the harbor.

After several of these nightly forays, it was learned that the Federals had deployed an elaborate system of chain booms around their ironclads which, in addition to being very dangerous for the submarine and the *David*, most surely would explode the torpedoes prematurely. In spite of this, Tomb continued his nightly missions into early January 1864, towing the *Hunley* well out past Fort Sumter on dark nights when the sea was relatively calm.

The submarine CSS *H. L. Hunley*. The towing of this innovative vessel almost ended in disaster for Tomb and the *David.*

Conrad Wise Chapman

On one of these nocturnal sorties, both the *Hunley* and the *David* came quite near meeting disaster. At some point in the tow, Tomb ordered the *David* stopped for an unexplained reason. As the two vessels sat gently rocking with the swells, the *Hunley's* torpedo came drifting up alongside. The towline became entangled in the torpedo boat's rudder assembly, and Tomb and Dixon watched in horror as the glistening black explosive canister, its sides bristling with Captain Lee's fuses, drifted closer and closer. The torpedo scraped against the side of the *David's* wooden hull and everyone held their breath. A crewman from the torpedo boat dived into the icy water, untangled the line, and pushed the torpedo away. It was a near miracle that both boats were not blown to pieces.

This would be the *David's* last tow of the *Hunley.* Tomb later recounted that after submitting his report, Commander Tucker refused to allow the torpedo boat to be put at further risk and canceled the towing operations.[13]

Meanwhile, construction on additional torpedo boats was progressing. In late January 1864, the Southern Torpedo Company launched two Davids at Charleston, and two Squib class boats were reported nearing completion at Wilmington while another David was under construction at Mobile. In February the War Department ordered Lee to build two additional Davids at Charleston, and construction of torpedo boats was also begun at Selma, Alabama and Savannah, Georgia. As news of all this building activity trickled out to the Federal Navy offshore, Union commanders became even more anxious and ordered increased vigilance among the monitors and blockaders of the fleet.[14]

A graphic depiction of the CSS *David*

Although Beauregard now had three Davids at his disposal, only the original *David*, commanded by Engineer Tomb, was completely operational. In addition to the towing operations for the *Hunley*, the *David* had been utilized in the month of January 1864, to lay floating torpedoes, but Beauregard was still intent on striking offensively at the enemy. On February 11, he wrote to Flag Officer Tucker suggesting that the *David* be assigned to duty in the Stono River. The Federals had removed the torpedoes that the Confederates had planted near the obstructions, and the USS *Marblehead* and USS *Pawnee* were now anchored at the mouth of the river. In addition, the USS *Memphis* was in the North Edisto River where she provided protection to Union barges that were busy ferrying troops and supplies across Schooner's Creek.

Tucker agreed with the commanding general, but because there were no pilots available who were familiar with the Stono, Tomb chose to attack the *Memphis*. Tomb selected two pilots, J. W. Cannon and A. Coste, who knew the North Edisto, and James Lawless went along as fireman. The *David's* captain wrote later of this attempt:

> On the 6th of March, 1864, the *David* made an attack upon the *Memphis* in North Edisto. Captain Theodore Stoney had a section of artillery to go down to the island by land to assist us. The night of the 4th we got near enough to the *Memphis* to see her lights, but our pumps failed to work and we returned up the river. The next night, about the same hour and spot, the pumps again failed to work. We made fast to the marsh, and after making repairs, again proceeded in the direction of the *Memphis*. About 12:30 a.m. [March 6], as we came within hailing distance, they hailed us, but we paid no attention to their hail, and the next moment they opened on us with small arms, the shot striking the steel cover did no harm. The next moment the *David* struck her on the port quarter about 8 feet below the surface. The blow was a good one, but the torpedo failed to explode. We then made a turn to port and came back at her, striking her on the starboard quarter. At this time the *Memphis* was going through the water at good speed and the blow was a glancing one, passing under her counter, taking a portion of our stack away, but the torpedo failed again to explode. Realizing we could do nothing more, we headed the *David* up the river. The *Memphis* at this time was using her heavy guns upon us, but they did not come near the *David*, passing well overhead. When we reached Church Flats and made an examination of the torpedo, we found the first blow was a good one, as the tube or cap on that side was mashed perfectly flat, and the glass tube containing the acid was broken, but being a defective tube it failed to explode. The second blow was not a good one, as the tube was slightly bent and the glass tube not broken. The expedition was a failure, caused by a defective tube. The torpedo held 95 pounds of rifle powder.[15]

The USS *Memphis* which Tomb attacked unsuccessfully
Official Records Navy

Upon learning of the attack and the failure of the torpedo to explode, Captain Lee was incensed and fired off an angry letter to General Beauregard, part of which read:

> As this occurrence may disturb the confidence heretofore felt in the torpedoes prepared by me, I deem it due to myself to state that about 10 days since I saw Engineer Tombs, and in the presence of Mr. Theodore Stoney, I distinctly told him that the torpedo then on the *David* could not be relied upon, it having been exposed for the last six months to every vicissitude of weather and climate. I further told him that I would furnish to the vessel a new torpedo, thoroughly tested, and that could be relied upon. Notwithstanding this advice, Mr. Tombs went on the expedition above reported without the slightest knowledge on my part, and carrying the old torpedo. Under these circumstances it is scarcely necessary to ask why the expedition proved fruitless....With the facts as above stated it may readily be determined whether the disaster may be most fairly attributed to a failure of the torpedo prepared by me, or to a willful disobedience to common sense instructions on the part of Engineer Tombs.[16]

Even though Stoney claimed he could not remember the exact conversation, Lee stuck by his story, maintaining that Tomb was negligent in using a torpedo that was certain to be defective.

Meanwhile, the building activity continued much to the consternation of the Federal commanders who kept receiving reports of the Confederate activity. A Southern deserter at Wilmington reported that two torpedo boats, the *Equator* and the *Yadkin* (Squib class), were nearing completion along with a David of nearly 150 feet.[17] On April 11, a Negro crewman,

Moses Bryan from the transport CSS *Rebel*, deserted to the Federal fleet at Charleston and reported that he had seen "two small torpedo boats and one large one, 150 feet long, which carries three guns; has a hole in her bow in order to fire a gun under the water. One of the small torpedo boats sank on Saturday, 9th, and they were trying to get her up at Chisolm's Wharf. Smokestack is 4 feet high, painted white."[18] Reports by deserters were notoriously suspect, but it is interesting that Bryan mentioned one torpedo boat at Charleston which was 150 feet long. This may well have been the CSS *Torch*.

Since March 14, when a reconnaissance party visited the mouth of the Ashepoo River and reported two enemy warships anchored there as blockaders, Beauregard had hoped to mount an attack utilizing several torpedo boats. The larger of the two ships was the USS *Wabash*, a 4,650-ton screw frigate mounting 45 heavy guns. Beauregard now had his opportunity. In mid-April of 1864, three torpedo boats left Charleston and threaded their way through various streams and tributaries finally reaching the Ashepoo River on April 18. Two of the boats were army and were commanded by Captains Augustus Duqucron and E. R. Mackay. The third boat was the original *David* commanded by Tomb. Unfortunately, the two army boats suffered engine problems and had to turn back, but the determined Tomb continued on alone. Later that night he headed for the *Wabash*.

At 150 yards he was spotted by one of the frigate's lookouts. Ensign Craven, officer of the deck, opened fire with musketry, beat the gong for general quarters, rang four bells for the engine room to start the engines, and ordered the starboard battery to open fire as soon as they were ready. The chain was slipped and Federal tars rushed to their stations as the giant warship, black smoke pouring from her funnel, began to move. The *David* was now only 40 yards distant when one of the starboard guns roared, sending a round shot splashing very near the torpedo boat. A second gun fired and the Union gunners believed they had scored a direct hit, for the dreaded torpedo boat had disappeared into the darkness.[19]

Although Tomb and the *David* were not hit as the Federal gunners supposed, he, nevertheless, was having his share of problems. The sea was rough and the *David* was taking on water faster than could be bailed. Even moderate swells swamped the cuddyhole, and water in the bottom of the boat was creeping up toward the boiler. Tomb decided it was too much and broke off the attack. Twice more, according to Tomb, he headed for the *Wabash*, but the heavy sea prevented his completing the attack.[20]

During the summer and into the fall of 1864, more Davids were completed at Charleston and one was nearing completion at Mobile. On May 2, 1864, three army Davids were ordered to proceed via inland waterways and attack the enemy's vessels in the waters of Saint Helena Sound and Port Royal. Theodore Stoney was put in charge of the expedition.[21] Again

The USS *Wabash*. Tomb was prevented from reaching her three times by heavy seas.

on May 24, Special Order Number 122 was issued from the headquarters of the Department of South Carolina, Georgia, and Florida:

> In pursuance to Special Orders, No. 122, paragraph II, from these headquarters, the army torpedo-boat No. 1, with the following crew, viz, E. R. Mackay, captain; Henry Mitchell, engineer; and William Baile, assistant engineer, will proceed to attack the enemy's fleet at any time that Capt. Theodore Stoney may direct.
>
> In pursuance to Special Orders, No. 122, paragraph II, current series, from these headquarters, the army torpedo-boat No. 2, with the following crew, viz, W. E. Fripp, captain; J. Forbes, engineer; and H. Steward, assistant engineer, will proceed to attack the enemy's fleet at any time that Capt. Theodore Stoney may direct.[22]

In September a deserter from the ironclad CSS *Chicora* reported to Federal authorities that he had counted eight torpedo boats in Charleston harbor alone.[23] On October 11, 1864, picket boats from the USS *John Adams* reported a torpedo boat off Sullivan's Island near Fort Beauregard. Seen also by the Federal lookout at Battery Gregg, the *David* was observed rounding Moultrie Point at daylight.[24] Union commanders intensified their anti-torpedo measures making it more difficult for any of the boats to conduct a successful attack. Nevertheless, the presence of these boats, the number of which were multiplied over and over in Federal commanders' minds, coupled with floating mines, obstructions, and the Confederate Navy's ironclads, posed an impassable barrier at Charleston over which the U.S. Navy refused to cross.

On September 28, 1864, Lieutenant General William J. Hardee
succeeded General Beauregard in
command of the Department of
South Carolina, Georgia, and Florida.
Beauregard, who had fought so hard
to convince the War and Navy Departments that the torpedo boat was
a viable weapon against the Federal
fleet, had been ordered to Petersburg,
Virginia, to oppose the Union advance on the south side of Richmond.
It did not take General Hardee long,
however, to appreciate the potential
of the torpedo boat judging from a
letter he penned on November 7, to
General Gilmer, chief of the Engineering Bureau in Richmond:

**Lieutenant General William J. Hardee,
CSA, who replaced Beauregard as
commander at Charleston**
Photographic History of the Civil War

I am very desirous of making
use of the torpedo boats finished
and being constructed by the En-
gineer Department on the coasts of South Carolina and Georgia for co-
operation with the forces under my command. It is better for many
peculiar local reasons that this new branch of the service should, in this
department, report directly to me, though I should desire that naval officers of experience and ability should command the flotilla. In organizing the corps I propose to select one officer to control the whole service,
who should make his headquarters in this city, one to command the flotilla on the coast of South Carolina, and one to command the Georgia
fleet. A number of officers are anxious to serve if the organization is perfected in the manner indicated. As the boats are being constructed under
your orders, I have thought proper to address this letter to you and ask,
if it meets with your approbation, that you will call on the honorable
Secretary of War and through him secure the action of the President in
this matter.[25]

Hardee's dream of a torpedo flotilla was not to be, however, for omi-
nous events were about to overtake the Confederacy. In a few more days
60,000 Union troops would leave Atlanta on a firey march of death and
destruction across Georgia and South Carolina. Charleston's days were
numbered, but it would not be the Federal Navy that would occasion the
fall of the South Carolina city. It would take General Sherman's troops approaching from the west to finally cause the Confederates to evacuate
Charleston.

There was one more drama to be played in the story of the Davids, but this would take place in Mobile, Alabama, not Charleston. The *St. Patrick*, a David similar to those at Charleston, was being built on contract to the Confederate government by John P. Halligan at Selma, Alabama. Part of Halligan's contract stipulated that as long as he was building the torpedo boat he was exempt from military service, and when the boat was complete, he would attack the enemy in Mobile Bay. The boat was scheduled for completion in July of 1864, but had experienced delays and General Dabney H. Maury, commander at Mobile, suspected that Halligan was not putting forth his best effort.

Major General Dabney H. Maury, CSA
The Confederate Soldier in the Civil War

The details concerning the *St. Patrick*—whether it was a David class torpedo boat or capable of total submersion as a submarine—are still shrouded in mystery. One Federal army officer claimed to have had inside intelligence concerning the boat being built at Selma. On April 12, 1864, Major General S. A. Hurlbut, commander of the XVI Army Corps at Memphis, wrote to Naval Secretary Welles:

> I am informed, and I believe credibly, that a submerged torpedo boat is in course of preparation for attack upon the fleet at Mobile.
>
> The craft, as described to me, is a propeller about 30 feet long, with engine of great power for her size, and boiler so constructed as to raise steam with great rapidity. She shows above the surface only a small smoke outlet and pilothouse, both of which can be lowered and covered. The plan is to drop down within a short distance of the ship, put out the fires, cover the smoke pipe and pilot house, and sink the craft to a proper depth; then work the propeller by hand, drop beneath the ship, ascertaining her position by a magnet suspended in the propeller, rise against her bottom, fasten the torpedo by screws, drop their boat away, pass off a sufficient distance, rise to the surface, light their fires, and work off.
>
> The torpedo to contain 40 pounds of powder and work by clockwork...One of the party has gone North for a magnet and air pump. I expect to catch him as he comes back. The boat is to be ready by 10th May.[26]

If General Hurlbut's information was correct, the *St. Patrick* could well be the most ingenious and innovative vessel of the entire war. It is doubtful that the torpedo boat referred to by the Federal general had all of those innovative features.

A second confirmation does exist, however, that the boat could be propelled by hand. On June 16, 1864, Commander Catesby ap R. Jones, commandant of the Confederate Naval Gun Foundry and Ordnance Works at Selma, had written to General Maury stating that the boat should be launched "in a few days." Jones went on to express great confidence in the boat explaining that it was powered by a very compact steam engine, but could be powered by hand while "under water." There were also "arrangements" for attaching a torpedo to the bottom of an enemy vessel. Whether all of this correspondence meant that the *St. Patrick* was indeed capable of total submersion, or just the capacity to lower itself up to the cuddyhole similar to other Davids, is still unclear.[27]

In spite of Jones' optimism, it was not until September that Halligan finally had the finished boat towed to Mobile. Unfortunately, even after his arrival he could not be induced to attack the enemy. Maury's patience wore thin and he had the boat transferred to the army and requested that Commander Ebenezer Farrand transfer Second Lieutenant John T. Walker of the navy to the *St. Patrick* as her commander. Walker, who had served on the cruisers CSS *Florida* and CSS *Georgia* in addition to the ironclad CSS *Chicora* at Charleston, was elated with the opportunity, but when he boarded the boat he found that Halligan had absconded with some of the necessary machinery. A search was instituted and Walker located the missing builder who was "comfortably established" in the Battle House Hotel in Mobile. Walker confronted Halligan, and as Maury diplomatically reported, "by energetic and good management," recovered the missing parts.[28]

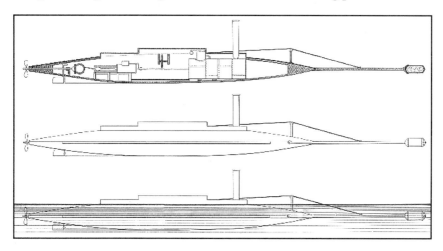

A sketch of a David class torpedo boat, purported to have operated at Mobile, Alabama

von Sheliha: *Treatise on Coast Defence*

The *St. Patrick* was 50 feet in length, 6 feet wide, and 10 feet in depth. A 12-foot iron spar, which could be raised and lowered from the cuddyhole, carried a copper torpedo at its extremity. Similar to other Davids, indications are that some form of ballast tanks allowed her to be raised and lowered while in the water. By January 27, 1865, Walker had her ready, and that night he steamed down the bay to attack the enemy fleet.

The navy lieutenant selected the gunboat *Octorara* as his target, and somewhere between 1:00 and 2:00 a.m., he began his run. Walker was still some distance astern when the *Octorara's* lookout spotted the torpedo boat and gave the alarm. The Federal vessel began to move as the lookout shouted, "Boat ahoy!" "Aye, aye," returned walker, while urging more speed from the engineer below. "Lie on the oars," commanded the lookout, thinking the David was a cutter. By this time the *St. Patrick*, a bit off course, rasped against the side of the *Octorara*, the torpedo not striking the hull, and for a moment the two vessels were locked together. The captain of the *Octorara's* deck guard, in desperation leaned over the rail, wrapped his arms around the torpedo boat's smokestack, and shouted for someone to tie her with a rope. Pistol shots whistled past his ears and he quickly let go. The *St. Patrick* disappeared into the darkness amid a hail of gunfire and returned safely to Mobile. There, engineers hauled her out of the water to repair machinery that had failed during the foray. The *St. Patrick* made no more attacks on the Federal fleet and was probably destroyed at the end of the war.[29]

The war would soon be over and both the Confederate Army and Navy husbanded their torpedo boats hoping for an opportunity to strike one more blow at an overpowering enemy. Southern commanders kept their boats in readiness to hurl themselves at the enemy should they try to break through the inner ring of defenses. In the end it was not the actions of the Davids and other torpedo boats themselves that kept the Federal Navy at bay, their mere presence was enough to do that.

The captain of the USS *Octorara* hangs onto the smokestack of the *St. Patrick* in this fanciful drawing by a *Harper's Weekly* artist.

Harper's Weekly

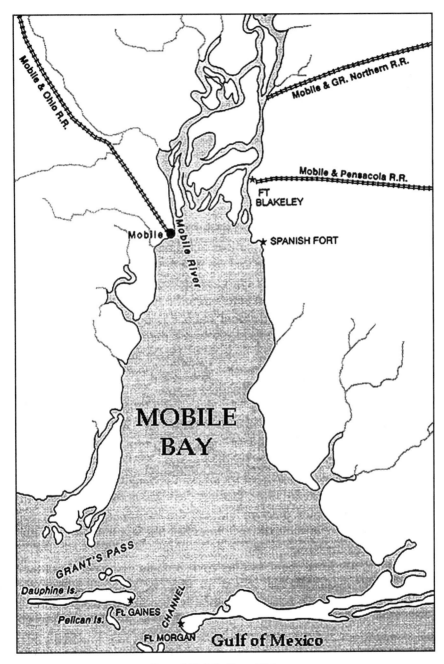

Map of Mobile Bay, Alabama

CHAPTER 7

THE CSS SQUIB

The account of the torpedo boat *Squib* is as much the chronicle of her captain, Commander Hunter Davidson, as it is of the boat itself. Without the daring and resourcefulness of an officer like Davidson, the Richmond-built torpedo boat would probably have been relegated to the obscure dustbin of history. Unfortunately, not very much is known about this courageous officer and the little boat that he used to attack one of the most formidable vessels in the United States Navy, but what is known will be presented here.

Born in Washington, D.C., in 1827, Hunter Davidson was appointed a midshipman in the U.S. Navy on December 29, 1841. Upon the opening of the Naval Academy at Annapolis, Maryland in 1845, Davidson was transferred to the school where he became a member of the second graduating class in 1846. Advanced to lieutenant, he had spent almost 20 years in the navy when just six days after the secession of Virginia he tendered his resignation to the Navy Department in Washington. All naval resignations that were submitted to the department after the firing on Fort Sumter, which had occurred on April 12–13, were not accepted, but rather the resigning officers were "dismissed" from the navy. Davidson was dismissed the same day as his resignation, April 23, 1861.[1]

Commissioned a first lieutenant in the Virginia Navy, Davidson, along with the rest of the state's naval personnel, was transferred to the Confederate Navy on June 10, 1861. His first assignment was to the Gosport Navy Yard at Portsmouth, Virginia, where, because of his experience in gunnery, he was put in charge of two of the broadside guns on the as yet uncompleted CSS *Virginia*. The ironclad *Virginia* was being constructed from the charred and sunken remains of the frigate USS *Merrimack* which the Federals had burned and scuttled when they evacuated Norfolk on April 20, 1861. Commanded by Captain Franklin Buchanan, the *Virginia* set out from Portsmouth on March 8, 1862, to do battle with the Federal fleet in Hampton Roads. The ensuing two-day engagement in which the *Virginia* destroyed

Commander Hunter Davidson, CSN

the wooden *Cumberland* and *Congress*, damaged the *Minnesota*, and dueled indecisively with the new turreted ironclad *Monitor* changed the course of naval warfare for generations to come. During the first day's fight one of the Dahlgren guns of Davidson's division had approximately two feet of its muzzle shot away, but the plucky lieutenant ordered his crew to continue firing.[2]

Buchanan was generous in his praise for his officers. His remarks concerning Davidson reflect the courage and determination that would characterize that officer's remaining Confederate service:

> Lieutenant Davidson fought his guns with great precision. The muzzle of one of them was soon shot away. He continued, however, to fire it, though the woodwork around the port became ignited at each discharge. His buoyant and cheerful bearing and voice were contagious and inspiring.[3]

Shortly after the Battle of Hampton Roads, Davidson was given command of the small gunboat CSS *Teaser* on the James River. The *Teaser* had been assigned to the Naval Submarine Battery Service, which was headed by Matthew Fontaine Maury who was now experimenting with torpedoes fired by electricity. Davidson and the *Teaser* were kept busy on the James during May and June as Maury planted numerous iron tanks filled with gunpowder near the batteries on Chaffin's Bluff below Richmond. The famous oceanographer was soon given an assignment overseas, however, and on June 20, 1862, Secretary Mallory sent an order to Davidson that, over the next three years, would enable him to become a leading expert on torpedoes and torpedo boats:

> You will relieve Commander Maury in the charge of devising, placing, and superintending submarine batteries in the James River, and you will exercise your discretion as to the ways and means of placing obstacles of this and any other character to oppose the enemy's passing of the river.[4]

Why Davidson was given command of this important operation is still a mystery, but he had evidently impressed Maury with his drive and intelligence while placing torpedoes in the James. The recommendation was probably put forward by Maury who gave him a glowing report, stating that Davidson had helped him "with a most hearty good will." President Davis, too, was impressed by Davidson, and characterized him as "an officer vigilant, fruitful in expedients, quick to perceive the defects incident to the application of a new engine of war, willing to admit errors, prompt in devising remedies, full of enterprise and intrepid in execution."[5]

Davidson set about completely overhauling the entire Naval Submarine Battery Service. In later years he would become obsessively protective of his achievements, claiming he alone was responsible for preventing the ascent of the James by the Federal fleet. Undoubtedly he did contribute greatly to Richmond's defense, and Davidson did much to advance the technology of torpedo warfare.

The means used in my electrical torpedo defenses differed in every essential particular from those used by Captain Maury in his experiments. The peculiar construction of the mines, the methods of fixing them in position and connecting them with the cables and batteries; the determination of the quantities of powder to use at different depths and the effective areas, the batteries used for firing, and also for testing the mines, as well as the organization and equipment of the stations from which the mines were controlled, all formed a complete system devised by myself.[6]

While Davidson was accomplishing this he still retained command of the *Teaser* and was about to come under enemy fire. During McClellan's ponderous Peninsula campaign the *Teaser* was utilized for the deployment of an observation balloon, one of the first such attempts in which the little gunboat could be called, with a slight stretch of the English language, the world's first "aircraft carrier." Later, Midshipman J. Thomas Scharf wrote of this experiment and the loss of the *Teaser*:

> Balloon reconnaissance was then practiced by both armies; and the *Teaser*, under command of Lieut. Hunter Davidson had gone down into Turkey Bend with a balloon on board, which it was proposed to send up in order that an observation might be made of McClellan's positions at City Point and Harrison's Landing. The *Teaser* got aground, and while thus situated was discovered by the Federal gunboat *Maratanza*, a ship carrying several 9-inch Dahlgren guns. Davidson could not retreat, so he opened fire upon the *Maratanza* with his two small guns, a 9-pounder and a 32-pounder rifle. He put a shot into the wheel-house of the *Maratanza*, but by her answering fire a shell was exploded in the boiler of the *Teaser*, and Davidson and his crew abandoned their vessel. They escaped to shore, but left behind them their balloon and papers that the Federals claimed contained valuable information, including particulars concerning the *Richmond* and her armament. [Construction of the ironclad *Richmond* was begun at Norfolk and completed at Richmond.] Lieut. Davidson, in reporting the loss of his vessel, requested a court of inquiry, which Secretary Mallory did not see fit to grant. "The Department," the Secretary wrote, "does not deem an inquiry as to the loss of the *Teaser*, by a court necessary, nor does it attach blame to yourself, your officers or crew in consequence thereof. Your conduct under the circumstances was judicious and creditable to the service."[7]

Davidson would continue the direction of the Naval Submarine Battery Service until near the close of the war when he was ordered overseas and was succeeded by First Lieutenant J. Pembroke Jones. It was during this period, sometime in 1863, the exact date having been lost to history, that a small torpedo boat was laid down at the Confederate Navy Yard across from Rocketts Landing at Richmond. The success of the *David* at Charleston had prompted orders for the construction of additional torpedo boats throughout the Confederacy, and the boat at Richmond, built by the navy, was in response to that request. Unfortunately, little is known about the vessel that would eventually be commissioned as the CSS *Squib*.

The designer of the *Squib* and three other Squib class boats built at Richmond, is uncertain, but it may have been Acting Naval Constructor William A. Graves. Several larger Squib class boats were designed by him later in the war and the *Squib* may have been his first effort. Graves had been granted a commission as an acting naval constructor on March 22, 1862, and served under the tutelage of Chief Naval Constructor John L. Porter in Richmond. The *Squib* was more conventional than the *David* having an open launch-type hull and a higher freeboard. In spite of her conventional appearance, however, she had a number of innovative and ingenuous features.

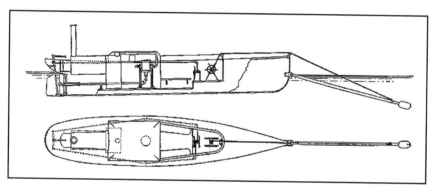

Detailed drawing of the CSS *Squib*

Official Records Navy

Launched in the early part of 1864, the *Squib* was often utilized as a flag of truce boat, and Captain John S. Barnes of the USS *Agawam* had ample opportunity to observe her as she passed up and down the James River:

> The boat is a propeller, of about 30 to 40 feet in length, of sharp model, moves rapidly under steam, and turns with great quickness. Her engine is covered with boiler iron, making a low, cupola-shaped, musket-proof house, which also protects the fireman, engineer, and one or two sitters. There is a washboard extending around the sides and covering the forward part, leaving an open cuddy for sitters and the pilot, who steers the craft with a small wheel. Upon the top of the stem there is a roller, or sheave, over which passes the guy to the torpedo staff and by which the torpedo is raised or lowered by means of a winch in the cuddy. On a stem at the water's edge is a goose neck, to which the torpedo staff is attached.[8]

The *Squib* was probably closer to 30 or 35 feet in length, was six feet in beam, and drew approximately three feet of water under her keel. Her machinery appears to have consisted of a small double-cylinder steam engine located amidships with the boiler, stack, and engineer's position aft. First Lieutenant William H. Parker, commandant of the Confederate Naval School, wrote that: "The engine was built in Richmond. I made several trips in this little boat, and when she was running at about half or three-quarter speed the engine made absolutely no noise."[9]

A propeller shaft ran underneath the boiler to a two-bladed screw which turned in a housing forward of the rudder giving the boat excellent maneuverability. Although no definitive reports exist concerning her speed, most accounts mention the fact that she appeared to be very fast. As Captain Barnes had observed, her vital parts were armored with boiler iron making her invulnerable to small arms fire. This covering also had the added benefit of providing protection for the crew.[10]

Meanwhile, Davidson had been experimenting in a laboratory near Richmond with an electrically fired torpedo attached to a spar of the Submarine Battery Services' latest vessel, aptly named the CSS *Torpedo*. The intent of his design was to carry the bulky batteries in a torpedo boat and close the contacts when the torpedo impacted the hull of an enemy ship. The difficulties of stowing the cumbersome batteries inside the hull of a small steamer, coupled with the uncertainty of closing the circuit at the exact moment the torpedo contacted the enemy vessel, led Davidson to discard the electrically fired weapon in favor of one fired by an almost

The CSS Squib under way in the moonlight

Courtesy of Dan Dowdey

exact copy of Captain Lee's chemical fuse. R. O. Cowley, electrician in the Naval Submarine Battery Service, described it in detail:

> The first thing to be done was to prepare a fuse which was not dangerous to handle, and which would explode quickly on contact with any substance. To this end we made some sheet-lead tubes, the rounded end being of much thinner lead that the other part.
>
> These tubes were about three inches long and one inch in diameter. Into this tube was inserted a small glass tube, of similar shape, filled with sulfuric acid, and hermetically sealed. The vacant space about the glass tube was then tightly packed with a mixture of chlorate of potash and pulverized white sugar, and the mouth of the lead tube was closed by fastening a strip of muslin over it.
>
> Now if the rounded end of the leaden tube is brought into contact with any hard surface, the thin lead will be mashed, the interior glass tube broken, and the sulfuric acid becoming mixed with the preparation of chlorate of potash and sugar, an immediate explosion is the result. We then prepared a copper cylinder capable of containing about fifty pounds of powder, and placed several of the leaden fuses in the head, so that no matter at what angle the butt struck the hull of a ship, one of the fuses would be smashed in, and flame from the potash and sugar ignite the powder. At the bottom of the copper cylinder there was a socket made to fit on the end of a spar.[11]

Davidson's first experiment with this type of torpedo involved the newly launched CSS *Squib*. An empty copper cylinder containing one of the chemical fuses was mounted on the 18-foot spar of the torpedo boat and Davidson rammed it into an old wharf at Rocketts Landing. Aside from denting the torpedo and severely shaking up Davidson and his crew, nothing happened. The canister was then filled with 25 pounds of rifle powder, and lowering the torpedo two feet beneath the surface, Davidson circled the *Squib* for another try. With a thunderous roar the torpedo exploded, pieces of timber and a geyser of water rose high in the air. The resulting cascade of water almost swamped the *Squib*, but when Davidson and his crew managed to back away they saw that the old wharf was a shambles.[12]

Davidson was now ready to attack the enemy. The closest enemy warships—at least at this stage of the war—were in Hampton Roads more than one hundred miles away by the twisting James River. One of the Federal warships on station there was the steam frigate USS *Minnesota*, the same vessel which had been involved in the two-day battle in Hampton Roads two years earlier. The 265-foot *Minnesota* weighed 3,400 tons, carried 47 heavy guns, and was on blockade duty in the Roads near Newport News, Virginia. By the beginning of April 1864, Davidson had made up his mind to attack her.

The USS *Minnesota*, Davidson's intended target in Hampton Roads
Naval Historical Center

The first step was to organize a small crew. Davidson was careful in his selection and chose only men he knew he could trust. Acting Master's Mates John A. Curtis and George W. Smith, both from Virginia, were selected with Smith being the senior of the two and probably acting as second in command. First Assistant Engineer Henry X. Wright was in charge of the engine assisted by First Class Fireman Charles Blanchard. Boatswain Thomas Gauley and Master William B. Hines, who acted as pilot, rounded out the crew.[13]

Davidson was now ready, but lacked one last essential—a supply of smokeless and spark-free anthracite coal. None of this valuable fuel was available in Richmond. Even the vessels of the James River Squadron had to burn soft bituminous coal which gave off sparks and clouds of black smoke. That would never do for a night attack on the Federals in Hampton Roads. Some enterprising soul, however, recalled that many prewar river steamers loading coal at the Richmond waterfront had used anthracite. Surely some of it must have spilled overboard. Divers were sent down and sure enough, a quantity of anthracite sufficient to fill the small bunker of the *Squib* was fished up from the river's bottom.[14]

With a 53-pound torpedo stowed on board, the *Squib* left Richmond sometime in the first week of April 1864. Davidson could not afford to use his precious coal, therefore the torpedo boat was towed down the James by a steamer, probably the CSS *Torpedo*. Traveling by night and hiding in various creeks by day to avoid any possible Federal patrol, the *Squib* arrived at

A photo of Rocketts Landing taken at the end of the war. The *Squib, Wasp,
Hornet,* and *Scorpion* were constructed across the river at the Navy Yard
which is visible over the roof of the large building in the foreground.

Library of Congress

a point approximately 15 miles below City Point, Virginia. Here she cast
off from the steamer and proceeded under her own power without incident, reaching a position on April 8, just above Newport News at the mouth
of the James. Wasting little time, Davidson planned his attack for later that
same night.[15]

After darkness fell, Masters Curtis and Smith busied themselves with
removing the torpedo from inside the boat and securing the weapon to the
end of the spar. At the same time in the stern of the *Squib,* Fireman Blanchard
began raising the fire beneath the small boiler. Engineer Wright kept a close
eye on the gauge as steam pressure inched slowly upward. Once the torpedo was ready Davidson checked the operation of the windless, making
sure he could lower the torpedo to the desired depth. It was a dark but
starlit night, and Davidson could easily discern the frowning Federal batteries on the left side of the river at Newport News. These would have to be
passed before he could reach the *Minnesota,* which was anchored in the
Roads. In addition, there were numerous other Union warships dotting the
waters around Newport News. They would have to be avoided at all costs.

Shortly after midnight, all was ready. With a nod from Davidson, Wright
started the engine and the *Squib* moved slowly out into the river. Pilot Hines,
taking advantage of the shadows on the south bank of the James, guided the
torpedo boat to the right side of the channel. Softly, Davidson gave the order
to open the throttle wide, and with no smoke and a muffled puff-puff, the
Squib steamed quickly out of the river and into the expansive waters of Hampton Roads. Davidson and his crew held their breath, but not one Federal
sentry on the Newport News batteries noticed their passage.

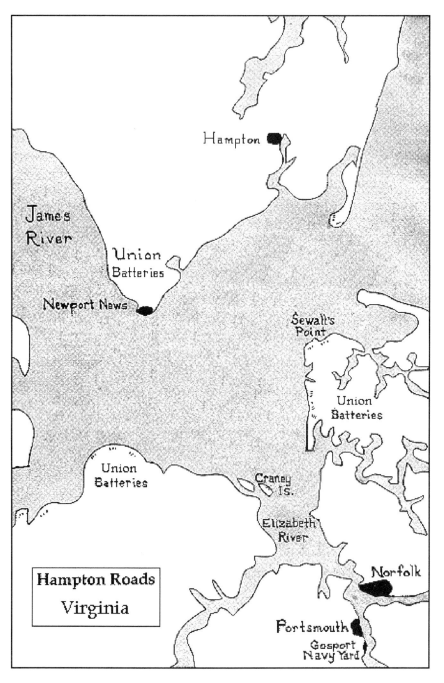

Map of Hampton Roads, Virginia

Carole Campbell, *The Powder Monkey*

Once in Hampton Roads Davidson's next concern were the numerous Federal warships, tugboats, and commercial craft that were anchored in the Roads. Throttling back to half speed, the *Squib* steamed silently through the maze of shipping, and although hailed several times, was not seriously challenged. The torpedo boat had often been utilized as a flag of truce boat during the day, and those Union lookouts who recognized her in the darkness paid little attention. Davidson knew the position of the *Minnesota*, and he slowly and carefully approached so as to put her off his port beam. It was a little before 2:00 a.m. when he finally signaled Wright to give the *Squib* all the steam she could handle.

Spinning the wheel, Davidson brought the helm hard a starboard and ordered another crewman to lower the torpedo. The sinister-looking black cylinder disappeared beneath the surface as Davidson pointed the knife-like bow of the *Squib* directly toward the looming black shape of the Federal man-of-war.

The torpedo boat was now knifing through the water at a tremendous rate, and everyone on board braced themselves as best they could for the expected explosion. At 150 yards, and closing rapidly, a challenge boomed out of the darkness. It was Ensign James Bartwistle, officer of the deck on the *Minnesota,* demanding to know the name of the approaching small vessel.

"*Roanoke,*" shouted Davidson hoping to buy a few precious seconds by masquerading as the Federal ironclad USS *Roanoke.* Bartwistle tried hailing the steam tug *Poppy* which was lying astern, ordering them to run down the intruder, but the engineer on the tug had let her steam go down and the *Poppy* could not move. Speaking through his megaphone, Bartwistle screamed for the onrushing boat to stay away and not to come alongside.

"Aye, aye," shouted Davidson.

Suddenly, as the *Squib* bore in, gun flashes erupted from the deck of the *Minnesota*—musket balls and pistol shots slammed into the torpedo boat. Davidson shouted for Wright to stop the engine. In the next instant, with a deafening roar, the torpedo exploded. The *Minnesota* trembled from bow to stern. Federal sailors went sprawling as loosened round shot scattered about the deck. "I never beheld such a sight before," wrote Master's Mate Curtis. "The air was filled with port shutters and water from the explosion, and the heavy ship was rolling to the starboard."[16]

The rattle was sprung, the drum beat to quarters, and Federal sailors poured out on deck. Fiery streaks of revolver and musket fire erupted along the rail as frenzied crewmen took aim at the ghostly shape of the torpedo boat which seemed to be drifting off into the darkness.

Meanwhile, Davidson and his men were having their own problems. When Wright reversed the engine it caught on dead center and now refused to budge. The *Squib* drifted helplessly as small arms fire rang against her armor. Wright grabbed an iron starting-bar and thrusting it into the flywheel, gave a mighty heave. With a burst of steam the engine was running again, and Davidson turned the boat away from the *Minnesota*. A heavy gun roared, splashing a shell almost under the keel of the fleeing *Squib*. Musket shots whistled by Davidson, some even tearing through his hat and clothing as he drove the speeding torpedo boat off into the night.

To mislead any pursuers, Davidson headed as though he intended to head up the Nansemond River, but at the last moment turned and disappeared up the James. Hiding in the marshes and creeks by day and being towed by the *Torpedo* at night, Davidson reached Turkey Island part way up the river two days later. There, he found a Confederate telegraph station and dispatched a jubilant message to Secretary Mallory:

> Passed through the Federal fleet off Newport News and exploded 53 pounds of powder against the side of the flagship *Minnesota* at 2:00 a.m., 9th instant. She has not sunk, and I have no means yet of telling the injury done. My boat and party escaped without loss under the fire of her heavy guns and musketry and that of a gunboat lying to her stern.[17]

The *Minnesota* was seriously damaged, but unlike the *New Ironsides*, not serious enough to cause her to be towed north to dry dock. Bulkheads were sprung, beams shattered, shelves and broken hull plates blown inward. Three 9-inch gun carriages were disabled and several elevating screws were bent rendering them useless. Rear Admiral S. P. Lee, commander of the North Atlantic Blockading Fleet, happened to be aboard the *Minnesota* the night of the attack. Furious that a torpedo boat had been allowed to approach the flagship, he sent word to Davidson that if the *Squib* was ever again used as a flag of truce boat she would be fired upon, for he did not consider such a vessel as being "engaged in civilized or legitimate warfare," regardless of her mission. Hunter wrote that "this glanced from my armor as many a worse shot did from my own side, though for other reasons, for I felt that as he was the sufferer then, he saw the matter from but one point of view, but that time would set it even...."[18]

The morning after the attack the Federals launched a search among the marshes and creeks that flowed into the lower James. A report that the mysterious torpedo boat had run into Pagan Creek, which flows down from Smithfield, was investigated on April 14. The USS *Stepping Stone*, towing several launches loaded with armed sailors and marines, steamed slowly up the creek and dropped anchor at Smithfield. Several army transports, which had followed, began unloading a detachment of troops. Suddenly the trees and bushes along the creek bank erupted in flame as a Confederate Signal Corps, which happened to be stationed in the area, opened fire. The Federals retreated, but not before one officer was killed and a seaman severely wounded. Acting Master D. A. Campbell, who was in charge of the expedition, later communicated to Admiral Lee the information he had gathered concerning the torpedo boat:

I am satisfied from the best information I could obtain that the rebel torpedo boat which has been hovering around these waters for a few days past left Smithfield on Sunday evening last bound to Richmond. It is reported by the inhabitants, with several of whom, both white and black, I conversed, and their statements all agree, the torpedo boat came to Smithfield on Saturday morning, the 9th instant, and left on Sunday evening for Richmond for repairs. As near as I could ascertain she is a wooden boat about 35 feet long, and very narrow, has a propeller engine, low pressure, is covered with boiler iron, making her shot proof against musketry, and is commanded by Lieutenant Davidson of the rebel navy.[19]

When Davidson arrived in Richmond, Mallory presented him to President Davis who was suffering from one of his chronic headaches. The president, displayed little enthusiasm for Davidson's exploit, irritably asking Mallory, "Why didn't he blow her up?" The chief executive soon joined Mallory in praising Davidson, however, and recommended that he be promoted to commander. The Confederate Congress made it official in June of 1864. Even Engineer Wright was advanced two grades for his quick thinking and efficiency in freeing the engine.

As the Davids had done at Charleston, the *Squib* spread alarm and in some cases fear in the Federal fleet stationed in Hampton Roads. Every ship in the fleet was ordered to maintain around-the-clock watches, and two small tugs were assigned to each warship with instructions to circle them continually at night. While the attack could be termed unsuccessful in that the *Squib* failed to sink the *Minnesota*, the Union vessel was damaged enough that she had to be pulled from her blockading position in order to undergo repairs. The ingenuity, skillfulness, and outright audacity of the attack was not lost on the Federal high command. The attack sent shock waves throughout the North, with the *Scientific American* commenting that "a little more practice will make them perfect."[20]

Sometime during the summer of 1864—the records are silent as to exactly when—the *Squib* was loaded on a flatcar and shipped by rail to Wilmington, North Carolina. There, after several crews trained on her in August, she operated in the Cape Fear River guarding against a possible Federal attempt to force a passage by Fort Fisher. One observer at Wilmington was not very impressed by the *Squib*. "It looks about the size or very little larger than some of the boats that belong to ships," he wrote. "It is a regular little steam propeller, has an iron rod projecting from the bow to which the torpedo is attached....I think anyone who would trust himself on board must have little regard for his own life."[21]

In Mallory's semi-annual report to President Davis dated November 5, 1864, he lists four warships as being on station at Wilmington, one of which was the *Squib*.[22] No other reports survive concerning her operations at Wilmington, though indications are that she may have ferried troops

President Jefferson Davis. The harried Confederate chief executive wondered why Davidson had not blown up the *Minnesota*.

and supplies to Battery Buchanan when Fort Fisher was under attack in January of 1865. In February, with the army's abandonment of Wilmington, the navy sank the *Squib* along with the *General Whiting*, a small steamer which had been imported from England and converted into a torpedo boat, at Point Peter on the Cape Fear above the city. The first of the Squib class torpedo boats was gone.

CHAPTER 8

THE "SQUIB" CLASS TORPEDO BOATS

The CSS *Squib* may have been the first true "Squib" class torpedo boat, but it was by no means the first small steamer to be fitted with a torpedo. With the success of the *David* at Charleston, army and navy commanders throughout the Confederacy sought ways to supplement their harbor defenses by adapting existing small steam-powered vessels with spar torpedoes. An example of this type of vessel was the CSS *Gunnison* at Mobile, Alabama. Slightly larger than the typical Squib class of torpedo boat, the 54-ton steamer was 70 feet long, 15 feet in beam and drew seven feet of water.

Originally known as the *A. C. Gunnison*, she had been built in Philadelphia prior to the war, and had been commissioned briefly as a privateer in 1861. Early in the conflict the Confederate government had issued letters of "Marque and Reprisal" to certain privately owned vessels authorizing them to prey upon United States commerce on the high seas. The *Gunnison* was issued such a letter at Mobile on May 25, 1861, and was commanded by her part owner, Captain P. G. Cook. There is no record of her sailing as a privateer, however, and sometime in 1862 she was acquired by the Confederate Navy, which utilized her as a tug and dispatch boat.

Because of her small size and powerful engine, Confederate naval authorities at Mobile decided to convert the *Gunnison* into a torpedo boat. Her upper works were covered over with boiler iron, and a 20-foot spar, which could be raised and lowered by a chain, was attached to the bow. At the end of the spar was a large 150-pound torpedo containing several of Captain Lee's chemical fuses.

On February 25, 1863, Robert B. Hitchcock, commanding officer of the Federal blockading fleet off Mobile, offered a fair description of the torpedo boat:

> She had a spar about 8 inches in diameter fitted forward, projecting 20 feet beyond her bow, secured between two ears by a bolt through the heel, but so that it could be moved vertically. The torpedo was of metal,

about twice the size of a powder barrel, elliptical in shape, with a socket in one extremity, into which was fitted the forward end of the spar, a clamp from the torpedo with a forelock through the eyebolt securing it in position. Inside the clamp were three bolts on the spar, one on each side for iron guys and one on top for a chain lift.

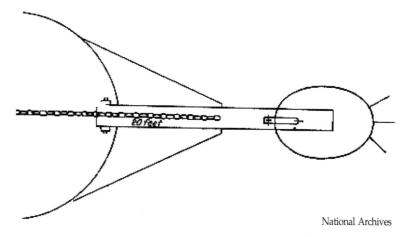

National Archives

The spar was usually kept in a vertical position, but when intending to use the infernal machine it was to be lowered below the water. On the forward part of the torpedo were three triggers diverging from a center point and laying parallel to the surface of the water; the machine was charged with 150 pounds of powder, and was to be exploded by a lock connected with the triggers.[1]

On November 9, 1863, Admiral Franklin Buchanan, commander of the Confederate squadron at Mobile, ordered Midshipman Edward A. Swain to relieve Acting Master's Mate F. M. Tucker of the *Gunnison*. Taking with him two experienced engineers, William M. Rogers and W. T. J. Kerrish, Swain was ordered to destroy "if possible" the USS *Colorado*.

Federal sources were aware of the *Gunnison* and her intended mission for on November 19, Lieutenant C. H. Green, who was misinformed concerning the *Gunnison's* captain, wrote to the commander of the Gulf Blockading Squadron:

> The steamer *Gunnison*, a small propeller, having a torpedo attached in a similar manner to the one used at Charleston, is about to run down the *Colorado* or such vessel as she may meet. She is commanded by one Cunningham, with a crew of not over ten men. She is iron cased about her boilers, carries no guns, has one smokestack, no mast, very low in the water, draws 7 feet. Torpedo contains about 150 pounds of powder.[2]

Swain prepared his crew for the attack, but discovered that several of the men had little enthusiasm for the mission and were replaced with eager volunteers. Federal sailors on blockade duty spotted the torpedo boat several times steaming within the confines of Mobile Bay, but just when all was ready Swain's engineers, who were also volunteers, refused to go. Buchanan, who considered the mission extremely risky, refused to assign a new crew, and the *Gunnison* spent the remainder of the war laying torpedoes and serving as a dispatch boat in Mobile Bay.[3]

The *Gunnison* was typical of many small steamers that were converted into torpedo boats throughout the South. With the success of the *Squib*, however, it became clear that to operate successfully against the Federal fleet, vessels built specifically for the purpose of torpedo attack were required. By November 1864, four Squib class torpedo boats were under construction at Richmond, one at the Peedee River Bridge in South Carolina, and two at Columbus, Georgia. Two boats, the CSS *Hornet* and the CSS *Wasp*, had already been completed at the Confederate Navy Yard across from Rocketts at Richmond, and would be joined early in 1865 by the CSS *Scorpion*. These three boats would serve valiantly with the James River Squadron until the end of the war.[4]

The *Wasp*, *Hornet*, and *Scorpion*, like the *Squib*, were most likely designed by Naval Constructor William A. Graves. The three boats were very similar, being larger than the original *Squib* at 46 feet in length and a little over six feet in beam. Each was equipped with an 18-foot wooden spar carrying a five-inch diameter torpedo, which could be raised and lowered from inside the armored cockpit. One of the boats was destined to eventually fall into enemy hands, and a chief engineer of the Federal Navy gave an accurate description on January 31, 1865, in a letter to his commanding officer:

> The machinery of the boat consists of two oscillating condensing engines of 7 inches diameter of cylinder and 6 inches length of stroke, of admirable workmanship, and so arranged that one person can manage both engine and boiler with the greatest facility. The boiler is of the ordinary tubular variety and very tight. She has fair speed for a boat of her kind, and is well adapted for the purpose for which she was built. The steering gear is forward, but there are no arrangements for permanently living on board.[5]

The history of the *Wasp*, *Hornet*, and *Scorpion* is closely entwined with the overall activities of the James River Squadron during the last year of the war. By late summer of 1864, Federal forces under the command of General Ulysses S. Grant had fought General Lee's Army of Northern Virginia in a series of sidestepping battles from the Wilderness, to Spotsylvania, to Cold Harbor, and were now across the James River where they encircled Richmond on the east and Petersburg to the south. Another army led by the detested Benjamin Butler, had threatened Richmond from the south, but with a ragtag group of soldiers, sailors, and marines, General Beauregard, hurriedly called from Charleston, had "bottled up" Butler's army in an area known as Bermuda Hundred.

The Union Navy had advanced its ironclads up the James as far as Trent's Reach where they had constructed a barricade of logs, chains, and sunken ships. Hundreds of large caliber guns, Confederate and Federal, now lined the river with the Federals controlling areas north and east, and the Southern forces arraigned along a line south and west of the river.

In January of 1865, the Union fleet in the lower James had been greatly reduced with most of the warships being sent to reinforce the massive attack which was about to take place on Fort Fisher at Wilmington, North Carolina. Secretary Mallory constantly urged Captain John K. Mitchell, commander of the James River Squadron, to take the offensive and attempt to capture Grant's huge supply base at City Point, Virginia. If this could be accomplished, the Federal Army of the Potomac might be compelled to withdraw its troops from in front of Petersburg. Only one U.S. ironclad remained below Trent's Reach, the double-turreted USS *Onondaga*, along with a few wooden gunboats.

The Confederate forces consisted of: three ironclads, *Virginia II*, *Richmond*, and *Fredericksburg*; the wooden gunboats *Hampton*, *Beaufort*, *Torpedo*, and *Nansemond*; the Squib class torpedo boats *Wasp*, *Scorpion*, and *Hornet*; and the armed tender *Drewry*. The *Torpedo* and the *Drewry* could also act as attack boats having been equipped with spar torpedoes. The Confederate Navy, Mallory stressed, would never again enjoy such superiority once the Federal vessels returned.

The winter of 1864–1865 was intensely cold, with a blanket of snow covering most of the ground. By mid-January heavy rains created freshets, or flooding, which played havoc with both the Confederate and

Captain John K. Mitchell, CSN, commander of the James River Squadron
Scharf: *History of the Confederate States Navy*

Union squadrons. On the night of January 14–15, 1865, Lieutenant Charles W. Read, commander of Battery Wood on the river just above Trent's Reach, observed large chunks of ice surging past his position. In addition, the next morning he thought he could see from a distance that some of the obstructions at Trent's Reach were gone. Read later wrote that:

> I sent two master's mates in a dugout down to examine the obstruction. After carefully sounding, the mates reported 14 feet of water through

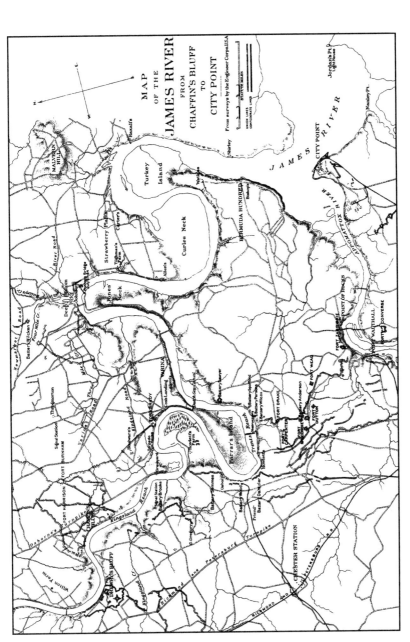

MAP
OF THE
JAMES RIVER
FROM
CHAFFIN'S BLUFF
TO
CITY POINT

From surveys by the Engineer Corps U.S.A.

STATUTE MILES

UNION LINES
CONFEDERATE LINES

Map of the James River from Drewry's Bluff to City Point, Virginia

Official Records Navy

the obstructions, of a width of about eighty feet. A boom consisting of a large spar lay diagonally across the entrance.[6]

A golden opportunity now presented itself, Read thought, for with most of the Federal monitors gone, there would most likely be little opposition to a vigorous Confederate thrust down the river. After receiving his men's observations and encouraged by their report, Read on January 15, hastened upstream to Drewry's Bluff where he penned an urgent message to Captain Mitchell:

> The net, which was stretched across the river above the obstructions in Trent's Reach, is gone. The schooner, which was sunk in the old channel on the south side, has drifted down several hundred yards. The vessel which was nearest the north shore has been drifted ashore abreast of her old position. The two vessels on each side of the north channel have lightened up by the stern; their entire sterns are out of the water; their bows are under the water. There is no vessel to be seen in the north channel.[7]

Read probably did not endear himself to his commander, for without waiting for Mitchell's reply, he immediately set out to inform army headquarters.

> I went at once to General Pickett's Headquarters and reported the results of our observations. General Pickett directed me to hasten to Petersburg and advise General Lee. General Lee asked if I thought the channel sufficiently wide and deep to admit the passage of the Confederate ironclads. I replied that I had no doubt of it, and that at any rate, it might be tried. General Lee ordered me to go at once to the Secretary of the Navy, and ask that the ironclads be sent down that night. I rode as fast as possible to Richmond and went to see Mr. Mallory and explained everything to him, and without the least hesitation he wrote an order to Captain Mitchell...directing him to move as soon as possible if he deemed it practicable.[8]

The following day, Mitchell was handed the urgent dispatch from the naval secretary:

> Since our interview I have heard nothing from you as to the enemy's obstructions in Trent's Reach, of which you thought you would be able to learn the condition. From Lieutenant Read I learn that the hulk which lay across the channel and the net also have been washed away, and I think it probable that there is a passage through the obstructions. I deem the opportunity a favorable one for striking a blow at the enemy, if we are able to do so. In a short time many of his vessels will have returned to the river from Wilmington, and he will again perfect his obstructions. If we can block the river at or below City Point, Grant might be compelled to evacuate his position. I can place additional officers and men at your disposal, should you require them for this great enterprise.

I hope you will be able to ascertain the condition of the obstructions and of your ability to force your way through them with reasonable certainty, and with such reasonable certainty as will justify this movement.

Should you move against the enemy, you will, of course, appreciate the importance of preventing the discovery of your design until its execution, and you will advise General Lee of your movements as well as the Department.

I regard an attack upon the enemy and the obstructions of the river at City Point to cut off Grant's supplies as a movement of the first importance to the country, and one which should be accomplished if possible.[9]

Mitchell answered Mallory on the same day, asserting that he needed more time in order to examine the obstructions more closely. He claimed that the freshet and bright full moon rendered a reconnaissance of the area impossible for the next several days. Evidently he was unaware that Read had already sent two of his own men to take soundings in the Reach, for Mitchell wrote:

Lieutenant C. W. Read informs me of the carrying away of the net above the obstructions and the shifting of some of the vessels. He does not state how or from whence these observations were made, but I presume they were not made on the spot, but from some point in our lines, and therefore too far to form a safe basis for calculation, though it may for speculation, as to other changes. Nothing but an actual inspection can be depended upon.[10]

Five days later, in spite of Read's reconnaissance and Mallory's urgent letter, the squadron had not moved. The naval secretary was persistent. On January 21, he wrote to Mitchell:

I have just sent a dispatch informing you that I expect you to start to-morrow. I do this because (I am) convinced that the enemy must learn your design and may defeat it, and because I regard the service which I am so solicitous about as of the utmost interest to our cause. You have an opportunity, I am convinced, rarely presented to a naval officer, and one which may lead to the most glorious results to your country. I deplore that you did not start immediately after the freshet, and have deplored the loss of every day since. I send Commander Wood to confer as to details, and to tell you what Captain Lee is doing for you, etc. You will, I trust, start tomorrow, and may Heaven make you and your squadron an instrument for the invigoration of our great cause.[11]

While Mallory continued to urge Mitchell to take the offensive, he added the following suggestion: "Would it not be well to give Read the command of all the small torpedo boats?"[12] Several telegrams must have followed, for later that night, Read was ordered to report to Mitchell for assignment as commander of the James River Squadron's torpedo boats.[13]

A painting of Lieutenant Charles W. Read, CSN, commander of the three torpedo boats of the James River Squadron

Oil Portrait by Pam Hardin

Read found the three boats anchored with the squadron near Chaffin's Bluff. The torpedo boat *Wasp* was commanded by Master's Mate Matherson, and Master Samuel P. Blanc commanded the *Hornet*. The third boat, the *Scorpion*, was in charge of Lieutenant Edward Lakin, who in July of 1864 had transferred to the navy from the Confederate Army.[14]

Fortunately, for the hesitating Mitchell, his Federal opponent was equally slow in reacting to intelligence reports concerning the obstructions and the expected movements of the Confederate fleet. Commander William A. Parker had assumed command in late November of 1864, when Admiral David D. Porter pulled most of the warships out for the projected attack on Wilmington.

Master Samuel P. Blanc, CSN, commander of the torpedo boat *Hornet*
Author's Collection

Only the double-turreted monitor *Onondaga* was left along with a handful of smaller wooden warships. The *Onondaga* was a formidable opponent, however, mounting two 15-inch Dahlgren smoothbores and two 150-pound Parrott rifles, the heaviest armament of any Union vessel in service. Parker's instructions when most of the fleet departed for Wilmington were to conserve his vessels and utilize them in patrolling the James from City Point to the obstructions at Trent's Reach. Parker's mindset, therefore, was on patrolling, and only if the Confederate vessels attempted to force their way down the river was he to engage them.[15]

Based on Read's report and pressured by the Navy Department to act, Mitchell finally moved his 11-ship fleet down to the Reach on the night of January 23–24. After enduring a heavy fire from Union-held Fort Brady while they floated by in the darkness, the Confederate-lead vessel arrived at the western end of Trent's Reach at approximately 9:00 p.m. Mitchell ordered the smaller *Fredericksburg* to attempt the passage first, and by 1:30 a.m., she had successfully negotiated the narrow channel and anchored 50 yards short of what was left of the Federal obstructions. Under continuous musket and mortar fire, Read again inspected the barrier and determined that there was 18 feet of water through the channel. The *Fredericksburg* and the *Hampton* passed through safely and anchored approximately one hundred yards below the entrance to the Dutch Gap Canal.[16]

Mitchell, who had accompanied the *Fredericksburg* through the barricade, returned upriver and found, to his "inexpressible mortification," that the *Virginia II* was hard aground. The *Nansemond* and the *Beaufort* struggled for three hours to free the big ironclad, but it was all in vain. Soon the *Richmond* was also aground, and the water in the river was falling rapidly. Mitchell, knowing that the Federal shore batteries would discover an easy target once daylight came, recalled the *Fredericksburg* and *Hampton*, and ordered the remaining vessels back to a sheltered stretch of river in front of Battery Dantzler. Much to his distress, the torpedo boat *Scorpion* and the tender *Drewry* could not comply with his orders as they, too, had run aground in attempting to free the *Virginia II.*

True to the Mitchell's expectations, at morning light the Federal batteries opened a blistering fire on the stranded Southern vessels. The range was only 1,500 yards, and the third shot from a 100-pounder Parrott gun penetrated the magazine of the *Drewry* and she exploded with a deafening roar. Fortunately, recognizing the vulnerability of the wooden warship, the officers and crew had been removed to the *Richmond* a short time before. Unfortunately, the force of the blast knocked the *Scorpion* free and she drifted down the river and was later captured. Shot and shell were raining constantly on the two ironclads, however most of them glanced harmlessly off their angled casemates. The *Onondaga* now added the weight of her massive 15-inch guns to the firestorm and the Confederate ironclads began to suffer from her fire.

Two heavy shells struck the *Virginia II.* One smashed into the port quarter, tore through the four-inch iron armor and two-foot thick woodwork,

The stranded Confederate ironclads are pounded by Federal guns at the Battle of Trent's Reach.

Harper's Weekly

and damaged the stanchions. The second shot broke entirely through the casemate, killing one sailor and wounding two others.

The *Richmond*, too, was hit several times and suffered damage to her stern by a shot from the *Onondaga*. At 10:45, with the water now rising, the *Virginia II* floated free and soon the *Richmond* was afloat as well. Slowly, the damaged ironclads joined their comrades back at Battery Dantzler.

Read and his three Squib class torpedo boats had been constantly under fire as they attempted to assist the grounded ironclads. Several days later, he submitted his report to Mitchell concerning his actions and those of the torpedo boats:

> On the night of the 23d instant, when the squadron proceeded down the river, the torpedo boats under my command were, in obedience to your orders, stationed in the following order: The *Hornet* on the port quarter of the *Fredericksburg*, the *Scorpion* on the starboard quarter of the *Virginia II*, and the *Wasp* on the starboard quarter of the *Richmond*.
>
> When the squadron passed the Point of Rocks the *Scorpion* was directed by you to cast off and sound the bar in Trent's Reach, and to examine the obstruction. Pilot Wood, of the *Virginia II* was sent with me in the *Scorpion*. We proceeded to sound the bar, but when we arrived at the obstructions the enemy opened upon us with musketry and a small mortar, and the pilot declined to sound farther, saying that he was satisfied that the channel was not open, and he became very insubordinate because I would not send him back to the *Virginia II*. I steamed up to the *Fredericksburg* and got her skiff and pilot. I then dropped the *Scorpion* down near the obstructions, and, taking with me in the skiff both pilots, I sounded through and across the north channel and examined the obstructions. I found 3 fathoms of water through the channel. A large spar was anchored diagonally across the channel, the upper end being secured to the sunken vessel on the south side of the channel and the lower end anchored near the middle of the channel; the spar was also anchored by the middle. I steamed up in the *Scorpion* to the *Virginia II* and reported the result of the examination to you. In obedience to your instructions I took two armed cutters and went down for the purpose of cutting the chains by which the spar across the channel was anchored. I conveyed to the commander of the *Fredericksburg* your order for him to get underway and push through at once. The *Fredericksburg* went through the obstructions before we had finished cutting the chains, but she did not strike the spar. You were then at the obstructions in a small boat, and ordered me to go on board the *Hampton* and run her against the spar, then to place a light on the vessel on the north side of the channel. I proceeded up in the *Scorpion*, but not finding the *Hampton* where she had at first anchored, I concluded that she had gone through, and I proceeded down in search of her, but it was so dark under the south bank that I could not find her. I did not look long, however, as I thought it best to get

a light on the obstructions as early as possible. I accordingly steamed up to the *Virginia II* for a lantern. When I reached the *Virginia II* I found her aground and was informed by you that the squadron would not go through that night. In coming alongside of the *Virginia II* the *Scorpion* was pushed against one of the *Virginia's* outriggers by a hawser which led from the starboard quarter of the *Virginia II* to the *Beaufort*. The torpedo pole and torpedo were carried away. The torpedo was towed ashore, secured, and delivered to the steamer *Torpedo*. When the *Scorpion* got clear I ordered her up the river to the *Richmond*. You directed me to get my boats under Battery Dantzler before daylight. I got on the *Hornet* and proceeded up toward the *Richmond*. Just below the *Richmond* the *Scorpion* was found aground. I endeavored to get to her in the *Hornet*, but could not on account of the shoalness of the water. I went up to the *Richmond* and ordered Master's Mate Matherson, in the *Wasp*, to go to the assistance of the *Scorpion*. The *Wasp* could not pull her off, but got ashore herself, but succeeded in getting off in a few minutes. I directed Lieutenant Lakin to use every exertion to get his boat afloat by daylight, but if he failed to get her off before that time to get his men out of range of the enemy's sharpshooters. Just as day was dawning I got the *Hornet* and the *Wasp* under Battery Dantzler.

When the *Drewry* exploded, the *Scorpion* was much strained and leaked badly. Lieutenant Lakin was severely, but I trust not dangerously, wounded. Firemen William Cooper and William Shailer were killed. G. W. Edwards was badly wounded and W. Council slightly wounded.

After dark on the 24th I proceeded down the river in the *Beaufort* for the purpose of towing off the *Scorpion*. It was blowing so fresh that the *Beaufort* was unmanageable. A small boat was sent to the *Scorpion* and found much water in her. The enemy turned his Drummond light on the *Scorpion* and his sharpshooters prevented us from getting to her again.[17]

On the same night that Read attempted to rescue his torpedo boat, Mitchell tried sending his squadron through the Reach again. The brilliant Drummond light that Read mentioned, also blinded the pilots of the ironclads and enabled the Union gunners to shoot almost as well in the darkness as in daylight. Mitchell halted his vessels and called his commanders together. Read, the junior of the officers present, argued in vain for an attack on the *Onondaga* at first light. "I advised an immediate attack on the monitor when we had the advantage of daylight to go through the obstruction," he recalled, "and could see when to strike the monitor with our torpedoes, as each ironclad had a ship torpedo ready for action, and when the pilots could handle the ships so as not to get aground again."[18]

Read's urging notwithstanding, Mitchell reluctantly ordered his battered squadron back to their anchorage near Chaffin's Bluff. Read's command was devastated. The *Scorpion* fell into the hands of the enemy, and two days later, on January 27, the *Hornet* collided with the flag-of-truce steamer *Allison* and the torpedo boat went to the bottom. It had been a humiliating fiasco. The Battle of Trent's Reach was over, and so was the last chance for the Confederate Navy to break through the Federal defenses and contribute to the possible relief of the siege of Richmond and Petersburg. Even more humiliating for the Confederate Navy's torpedo service was the loss of two of their three boats. Unfortunately, in April, the *Wasp* too would be lost, and the remaining boats being constructed at Richmond would not be finished in time and would have to be set ablaze when the city was evacuated.

While the James River Squadron had been successful in integrating torpedo boats into their operations, other points in the Confederacy had not been so fortunate. Begun with high hopes and expectations of rapid completion, most boats languished on the way for lack of materials, machinery and skilled mechanics. As the war ground into its finale year the Confederacy's worn-out rail system made it even more difficult to get engines, iron plates, shafts, propellers and the hundreds of other boat building materials that were needed delivered to the construction sites. In some cases boats had to be abandoned or destroyed with the approach of the enemy.

And then, ill fate itself sometimes lent a hand. At Wilmington, North Carolina, a fire broke out at the cotton yard on Eagle Island. The flames spread quickly from the warehouses along the Wilmington and Manchester Railroad, engulfing 25 railroad cars, large quantities of stored cotton bales, a good portion of the wharf and the government cotton press. The flames also reached the Beery Shipyard where they consumed the saw mill, large amounts of cut timber, and two army David class torpedo boats as well as a Squib class navy boat. All three vessels were just days short of completion.[19]

It was now becoming painfully evident that the Confederacy did not have the resources nor the facilities to construct enough torpedo boats to seriously challenge the growing number of Federal warships encircling her shores. The only viable option was to have them built overseas. On July 18, 1864, Secretary Mallory wrote to the navy's purchasing agent in England, Commander James D. Bulloch:

> Experience has shown us that, under certain conditions, we can operate effectually against the enemy's blockading fleets with torpedo boats; and I desire that you will send six of them as early as practicable. Enclosed herewith you have the drawings of a class of these boats, designed by Constructor Graves, together with a general description of their machinery by our engineer in chief, Mr. Williamson; by which drawings and description they may be built. Should you, however, upon conferring with experts, deem any change or variation of plan expedient, you are at liberty to build three of the six according to your own views, the other three upon the plan enclosed. As these boats select their own time for operating and

may thus secure a smooth sea, and as they must operate at night and avoid being seen, it is important that they should be as low in the water as way be consistent with their safety. They are expected to carry from five to seven men, coal for twenty-four hours, and four torpedoes with their shifting poles, and to go at least 10 miles an hour with all on board. The arrangement of the torpedo is quite simple. An iron strap like this—

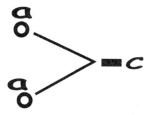

Official Records Navy

is fitted to the bow of the boat, the bolt upon each side, *A A* being about 4 or 5 feet abaft the stern post. At *C* the strap forms a socket large enough to receive a light spar six inches in diameter, a hole being drilled through the socket to correspond with one through the base of the pole, through which a pin secures it. The appearance of the boat will then be this:

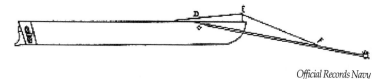

Official Records Navy

The torpedo is usually made of copper or iron boiler plate, contains from 40 to 100 pounds of powder and is prepared with three sensitive tubes which explode it by impact. Its effect depends mainly, of course, upon its depth below the surface, and upon its being in immediate contact with the side of the vessel struck.

The torpedo boats are miniature swift steamers, and they must be strongly built of good iron and as light as may be consistent with strength, and particularly strong forward, as they may sometimes run into a vessel. *D E F* is a line leading over a stanchion, which stanchion should be made to lie horizontally when not in use, to hoist the torpedo spar out of the water.

They require no berths or other accommodations for sleeping. If two screws could be introduced their ability to turn, an important advantage, would be improved.

I suppose these boats could be built and sent to us without interference by the authorities; but if not they might be built in sections and thus sent over. We are so destitute of mechanics, however, that they should be sent us complete as possible, and with each boat six caissons or torpedo boxes, according to the plan enclosed.

It would be prudent to conceal from those who make the boats and boxes the use to which they are to be applied.[20]

Bulloch replied to Mallory's request on September 16, stating that all six boats had been contracted for, and that the plans had been placed in the hands of the builders. Three of the boats were to be built on the lines of

Graves' plans with only slight modifications to strengthen the stem and change the rake of the stern. The other three would be slightly larger in order to accommodate larger boilers. Constructed of light steel, the boats with engines, boiler, water in boiler, screws and shafts, coal for 24 hours, three torpedoes and a crew of five, were calculated to weigh 9.18 tons. Draft would be only three feet and their speed was intended to be greater than 10 knots. As far as can be determined these boats were completed sometime in January or February of 1865, but it is extremely doubtful if any of them ever reached the Confederacy.[21]

Commander James D. Bulloch, the ingenious purchasing agent for the Confederate Navy in Europe
Scharf: *History of the Confederate States Navy*

Engines, too, were constructed in England. Even before Mallory ordered the six boats from Bulloch he had sent a request for 12 small marine engines for use in torpedo boats. Bulloch ordered these from the Clyde Bank Foundry in Glasgow, Scotland, and all were completed and shipped in three blockade runners around September of 1864. Whether any of these engines reached their destination is unclear, but some may have found their way into some of the last David class or Squib class boats built in the Confederacy.[22]

The last service performed for the Confederacy by a Squib class torpedo boat appears to have been carried out by the CSS *Viper* at Columbus, Georgia. Two Squib class boats designed by Graves were begun at the Confederate Navy Yard at Columbus, but only the 45-foot *Viper* was completed before the end of the conflict. She was launched on March 31, 1865, but by this time the enemy was advancing on Columbus. By April 15, Union General James H. Wilson's army, after destroying the army and navy facilities at Selma, Alabama, was only 12 miles away. The following day, Easter Sunday, ragtag Confederate forces fought a delaying action throughout the afternoon and evening, but time was quickly running out.

Dutiful to the end, an unnamed but courageous Confederate clerk filled out the last entry in the navy yard log:

Sunday 16   Easter Sunday—weather pleasant—The excitement in town intense—Began early this morning loading stores on *Chattahoochee* and *Jackson*—about noon sent the *Chattahoochee* off in tow of the "Young" in charge of Master Vaughan—About 2 p.m. a smart skirmish occurred at lower bridge which was burned by our forces. Firing also at upper bridge which continued an hour or two. About 8 p.m., heavy firing at upper bridge which lasted until between 9 and 10 when the enemy broke thru our lines and obtained possession of the bridge and City. Our forces leaving as rapidly as possible.

About 9½ Lieut. McL ordered all the officers at the Yard on board the Torpedo [*Viper*] to proceed down the River—Excepting himself, clerk, and Dr. Stoakley who retreated by the land route and were captured by the enemy.

Neatly and carefully inscribed below this last log entry is one word: FINIS.[23]

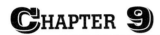HAPTER 9

A DESPERATE MISSION

Excerpted from *Sea Hawk of the Confederacy* by the author.

The failure of the James River Squadron to force its way downstream and attack the huge Federal supply base at City Point was a bitter disappointment for the Confederate Navy. To make matters still worse, it had lost the tender *Drewry* and two of its three Squib class torpedo boats. No doubt Charles Read was convinced that if Mitchell had acted swiftly upon his report that the obstructions had been washed away, the ironclads and his torpedo boats could have raised havoc with the Federals. Maybe, just maybe, the destruction of the supply base at City Point would have necessitated the withdrawal of the massive army in blue that encircled Richmond and Petersburg. But now with the fall of Fort Fisher, the enemy's ironclads would soon return, and it would be impossible to launch another attack with any hope of success.

For several weeks, even before the aborted attempt at Trent's Reach, Read had been pondering another method of attacking Grant's supply base. With the knowledge gained from the small commando raids, and with the advent of the failed operations at Trent's Reach, he now took his proposal to higher authorities. With men from the James River Squadron, Read's plan was to transport four launches overland on wagon frames, which would travel southwest out of Petersburg and around General Grant's left flank. By this route he felt sure he could gain the rear of the Union army without being detected. Once behind the Federals, he would turn his column east and continue on a course that would take them completely around the Union forces. His objective would be to cross the Blackwater River and attempt to arrive at the James River somewhere in Surry or Prince George County.[1]

Upon reaching the river, Read planned on concealing his command along its marshy banks until an opportunity presented itself to capture one or more of the Union steam tugs that were constantly passing up and down

An autographed photograph of Lieutenant Charles W. Read, CSN, taken two years after the war.

the river. Perhaps, he argued, they might even be able to seize a Federal transport lying at anchor in Burwell's Bay. After seizing the Union vessels, they would affix torpedo spars and torpedoes to the tugs and steam up the river to attack the Union vessels at City Point. At the same time, upon a given signal, Mitchell would attempt again to force his way down the James with his ironclads and join in the attack. A desperate mission, perhaps, but Read was convinced that it was time for such desperation.

Mitchell and Secretary Mallory gave their approval, and on February 1, a group of naval officers and 90 to 120 men (estimates vary) from the James River Squadron were assigned to Read "for temporary special duty." The officers included Lieutenants William H. Ward, William H. Wall, and John Lewis; Masters W. Frank Shippey and John A. G. Williamson; Acting Master's Mates William McBlair and James T. Layton; Midshipmen James A. Peters and Henry H. Scott; and Pilots E. C. Skinner and James Turner. The marine contingent of 13 men was under the direction of First Lieutenant James T. Thurston, CSMC. Five assistant engineers and five first class firemen were also ordered to report to Read. They would be needed to operate the engines of the captured Federal vessels.[2]

Friday, February 3, 1865, dawned bitterly cold and overcast in Virginia. For the Confederate sailors and marines stumbling into formation at

Midshipman James A. Peters who accompanied Read on his desperate mission behind enemy lines

Author's Collection

Master John A. G. Williamson, another officer on the trek to the Blackwater River

Naval Historical Center

Drewry's Bluff, it must have seemed especially dreary. These were some of the same men who only a few days before had seen their navy's attempt at Trent's Reach fall apart when the two ironclads went aground. A few of the shivering sailors in the ranks may have come from the two torpedo boats which had been lost. They all understood how desperate the military situation had become for the Confederacy. They also knew that much would be expected of them.

No official record of Read's expedition, if one was ever written, is known to have survived, but history is indebted to Master W. Frank Shippey, the commander of the small gunboat CSS *Raleigh* who had been assigned to the mission. Shippey kept a log during the expedition, and he wrote of the many dangers that they expected to encounter:

> The expedition was a hazardous one from its incipiency, the enemy having declared their determination to show no mercy to prisoners taken on torpedo service. We had to operate in the rear of Grant's army—a handful of men, with an army of one hundred and fifty thousand between us and our friends—and every man on the expedition fully understood and appreciated the danger we ran. If we were successful in reaching the James River our dangers would have but just commenced, as we would have to board and capture an unsuspicious craft, of whose fitness for our purpose we would have to judge from appearances at long range; the capture might attract attention of the men-of-war and make us the captured instead of the captors, or our plan discovered, we would have a long way to retreat in order to reach a place of safety. Added to these difficulties, the weather was very cold, the roads rough, and the path before us a 'terra incognito.'[3]

That Read was confident of success, was illustrated by one of his letters written to a member of the expedition not long after the war:

> I am sure before they could possibly have known what was going on I could have run alongside and boarded a gunboat with my men, and, having thus captured the first gunboat, with this gunboat and my torpedoes, I could easily have sunk the rest of the gunboats...My plans were made known to General Lee, and were also approved by President Davis himself.[4]

The Navy and Marine Corps veterans shivering in ranks on that bleak February morning had seen almost four years of war. Now, they were being asked to produce a miracle for the struggling Confederacy. With the inspection of their arms and equipment completed, four heavy wagons, each pulled by four mules, were driven up in front of the assembly. The wagon beds had been removed, leaving only the frame, axles, and wheels. A whaleboat was chocked in place onto each wagon frame, and spars, torpedoes, rations, and various other provisions were loaded and secured on board the boats.

In mid-January, Lieutenant John Lewis had been dispatched to reconnoiter the country and the route that Read intended to take. Lewis' instructions were to meet the contingent at a ford on the Blackwater River, southeast of Petersburg, where he would guide them on to the James. With inspections concluded and everything loaded, Read and his men were ready to move out.[5]

Taking the rough frozen road south, the caravan left Drewry's Bluff, heading for Petersburg on February 3, 1865. Read, along with his second in command, Lieutenant William H. Ward, took the lead with all of his sailors. Because most of these were crewmen from the ironclads that patrolled the James, marching over the winter roads would not be easy. Some may have reflected that serving on an ironclad warship in winter with steam up, while boring duty, meant that at least they could stay warm. About one hundred yards behind the sailors, came the wagon train commanded by Master Shippey, whose logbook contains the only complete account of this naval expedition. Behind the wagons, and acting as a rear guard, came the detachment of Confederate marines.

It is interesting to speculate on what the grizzled and hardened veterans of the Army of Northern Virginia must have thought as they witnessed

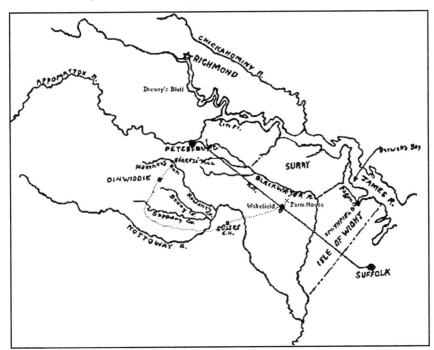

The dotted line on the map traces the approximate route taken by Read and his command.

Author's Collection

this strange procession. Trudging along the frozen road through their midst were men in sailors' uniforms armed with cutlasses and revolvers. Mule teams dragged their boats behind them, followed by gray-coated marines carrying knapsacks and muskets—a strange sight indeed.

The weather, after such a gloomy beginning, had become bright and sunny, and the men made good time over the frozen Virginia roads. Arriving in Petersburg, Read turned his command southwest out the Boydton Plank Road. By evening, they had reached General Richard Anderson's headquarters on the right flank of the Confederate lines southwest of Petersburg. The men encamped for the night, and Read was satisfied that the first day had been a good beginning.[6]

The following morning, February 4, the expedition left Anderson's lines and continued trudging along the Boydton Plank Road. After a few miles they passed through the Confederate picket line, and they were now very much on their own. No Union troops were encountered as the Federal picket line had not yet been stretched this far west. About 10 miles southwest of Petersburg, just past Burgess Mills, Read turned his command toward the southeast. Keeping to unfrequented rural roads, the tired sailors and marines marched another 14 miles before halting for the night. They were now well behind the Union lines. Fortunately, no Federal stragglers or foraging parties were encountered. Shippey recalled this first night behind enemy lines:

> We were now fairly embarked on our expedition, pushing our way through the enemy's country and separated from our friends by his army. Indeed, we were out of the line of travel, the Federals did all their business at City Point, and there was little more to attract anyone to this part of the country than to the Siberian deserts.[7]

With high spirits and aching muscles, the men bivouacked for the second night.

Getting an early start the next day, Sunday, February 5, Read pressed his command forward over the rough country roads. The weather was clear and they made good time. Occasionally, someone would give an alarm that "Yankees" had been spotted, and the whole command would take to the woods. Fortunately, these all proved false, and they continued to move on. The wagon wheels clattered over the frozen ground as the sailors and marines, not being accustomed to long marches, began to feel the pain. At 9:00 p.m. that night they made camp, having covered an estimated 30 miles—a good day's march even for seasoned troops. When they built their campfires that night to cook their meager rations, it was with the realization that they were now deep within enemy-occupied territory.[8]

The following day, February 6, was uneventful, and other than an occasional alarm which again caused the command to take cover in the woods, they moved along at a steady pace. With the weather continuing cold but fair, they covered 15 miles before camping near Wakefield Station on the old abandoned Norfolk and Petersburg Railroad. They were now southeast of Petersburg, and the Blackwater and James Rivers were not much farther ahead. One more day's march and they would be at the banks of the James. The excellent weather which they had the good fortune to experience, however, was about to change. The night turned bitterly cold and toward midnight it began to snow. The men huddled closely around the fires in a futile attempt to keep warm...so close in fact that one of the junior officers, John A. G. Williamson, had a lively brush with "disaster." Shippey recalled with amusement:

> He was lying close to a fire, and as I passed about midnight I saw that his coat-tail was on fire, and called him somewhat hurriedly from a sound sleep. He started up and rushed wildly through the woods, the fiery tail streaming out behind, and for awhile all efforts to stop him were futile, but we finally succeeded in capturing him, extinguishing the fire with the loss of one skirt of his coat. He afterwards cut off the other skirt and made it more 'uniform.'[9]

As the gray morning light broke over the bleak and frigid Virginia landscape, the scene was truly miserable. It had snowed heavily since midnight, and was now alternating between snow, sleet, and freezing rain. As the shivering sailors and marines crawled out from under their blankets, they discovered that everything which had been exposed to the elements was covered with a thick coating of snow and ice. Breaking camp, the expedition assembled in the road, and braving the storm, they began to move out. Each man, along with the wagons, took up his assigned position in the line, but progress was slow because the mules had difficulty pulling the heavy wagons on the slippery road.

As they struggled along, the wind gradually increased until it became a howling gale. Visibility was nil. Men and animals, their heads bent against the shrieking wind, became blinded by the driving sleet and little headway was made. Time and again a mule team would fall or a wagon would slide into the ditch along the road, blocking the way for those behind. With sleet stinging their hands and faces, the half-frozen sailors struggled to push the heavy wagons back onto the icy road. Once they had succeeded, the column would again move on slowly. After two hours of this pain and frustration, Read ordered the command to halt and take shelter from the raging storm in a nearby abandoned farmhouse. They were now only a few miles from their rendezvous with Lieutenant Lewis on the Blackwater River.[10]

Securing the mules behind the house and away from the biting wind, the men crowded inside where fires were built in the large stone fireplaces. Huddled around the smoky fires, they began thawing out and drying their clothes. Read, impatient to continue, paced the floor and decided that as soon as the storm subsided they would press on. While they waited and listened to the howling elements whistling around the corners of their dilapidated shelter, crushing and inconceivable news arrived. Someone called out to announce that a rider was approaching, and as Read stepped outside an exhausted gray-clad soldier rode up on a weary horse. The man was nearly frozen in the saddle and had to be helped from his mount and assisted inside. With anxious faces gathered around, he began to tell a tale that was almost inconceivable.[11]

The nameless Confederate related how he had been a prisoner of war at Fort Monroe, Virginia, and on one of the long, dreary days of his imprisonment, he had overheard from his cell window a conversation between a Confederate naval officer and his guards. The officer informed his captors of a planned overland torpedo expedition to the James River, and even offered to lead a Federal infantry regiment to the crossing of the Blackwater where they could ambush and capture all those involved. The Confederate naval officer whom he had overheard, he claimed, was Lieutenant John Lewis.

Escaping from Fort Monroe shortly after this eavesdropping, the young soldier was determined to find the naval expedition and warn them of the awaiting danger. Read was stunned. He simply could not believe this story of betrayal. Lieutenant Lewis, although Northern-born, had served the Confederate cause faithfully since the beginning of the war. Being in the United States Navy and stationed at Norfolk when Virginia seceded, Lewis had resigned and joined the Confederate Army. Wounded at Manassas, he later resigned from the army in order to accept a commission on June 29, 1864, in the Confederate Navy as a first lieutenant. During the latter part of 1864, he had served on the CSS *Drewry* on the James River and the ironclad CSS *Albemarle* in North Carolina. Read was positive Lieutenant Lewis' loyalty was above question.[12]

There was only one way to determine if the young soldier was telling the truth; Read would have to go and see for himself. After a council with his officers, and fearful that they might be discovered in the farmhouse by Federal foraging parties seeking shelter from the storm, Read decided to take the men and boats back down the road about a mile and conceal them in the woods. If he was not back by sundown the following day, it would mean he had been captured. In that case, Lieutenant Ward was to turn the command around and attempt to regain Confederate lines by retracing their route.

The men, reluctant to leave the warmth of the fireplaces, nevertheless filed out, hitched up the wagons, and began to retrace their steps. After backtracking what Read considered to be a safe distance from the farmhouse, the command turned off the road and made camp in the dense woods. The wagons were hidden and their tracks eradicated by utilizing tree branches. Putting on a "disguise" (probably a civilian overcoat) as Shippey described it, Read mounted his horse and set out on the lonely ride. Hopefully, he must have thought, he would prove the young soldier wrong.[13]

Although the sleet and snow had stopped, it had turned bitterly cold. The frigid wind howled through the forest causing tree limbs to crack and break under the heavy load of ice. Falling branches and chunks of ice became a real hazard for both men and mules. Because of the possible proximity of roving Federal cavalry patrols, Ward dictated that under no circumstances were campfires to be lit. The cold, windy night passed drearily by, while the men huddled together in a feeble effort to keep from freezing to death. When the long-awaited morning light finally broke over the eastern horizon on February 8, Ward ordered the men to remain hidden and out of sight in their secluded patch of woods. Worried over their leader's whereabouts, the cheerless day dragged by, and still the men saw no sign of Lieutenant Read. Shippey wrote that, "the following day, though but a short winter one, seemed endless, so great was our anxiety for our leader, who had thrust his head into the lion's jaws."[14]

Anxiously, the men kept watch for their commander's return. At around 4:00 p.m., Read came riding down the road and turned off into their hiding place. His innermost fear had been confirmed; there was an ambush waiting at the Blackwater, and the Union cavalry was already out scouring the countryside searching for the torpedo boat expedition. If they had not been slowed by the violent storm, he explained, they would have certainly blundered into the ambuscade and been killed or captured.

As an aside to this narrative, there is an interesting record in existence at the U.S. National Archives. The records of the Headquarters Detachment, 3rd New York Cavalry, show that a "Lieutenant Lewis of the C.S. Navy" was forwarded from Benvard's Mills, Virginia, to Portsmouth, Virginia, on January 20, 1865. The remarks section of this record state, "A deserter from the C.S. Navy, Lt. Lewis has horse & equipment." Evidently, the Federals did not trust him to lead the ambush, for he was forwarded from Fort Monroe to a prison in Washington, D.C., on February 4, 1865.[15]

Read knew that they had only two choices: they could either surrender to the Federal cavalry, or turn back and attempt to pass around the rear of Grant's whole army again in order to gain the right flank of the Confederate lines. With surrender being unthinkable, there was no hesitation, and the order was given to hitch up and move out. They had come approximately 85 miles, and now they had to retrace those same miles to reach the safety of Confederate-held territory. Avoiding the main roads that were patrolled by enemy cavalry, Read led his command along deserted and little-known farm traces. They marched all night, and concealed themselves during the daylight hours of February 9, to prevent being spotted by the Federals, who now seemed to be everywhere. The following night, the march was cautiously resumed. Every road seemed to be guarded by Federal pickets, and with hands nervously fingering their revolvers, the men carefully moved on. Unexpectedly, an elderly gentleman, who was a resident of the area, approached the group and offered to be their guide. With little to lose, this offer was accepted and they continued the march. Traveling by night and hiding by day, and following the old man in the "stove pipe hat," as Shippey described him, the command kept moving westward. Taking a more roundabout route, they proceeded by way of Sussex Court House, Stony Creek, and then to Dinwiddie Court House.

Approaching either Stony Creek or the Nottoway River (Shippey mistakenly referred to the Appomattox River, but that stream was well within Confederate-held territory), they found that the only way to cross, was by fording. The temperature was hovering around the freezing mark, and the stream was covered with a thin coating of ice. With Union cavalry sniffing at their heels, they plunged into the chest-high water and pushed across. Shippey recalled:

> It was not a pleasant prospect, that of taking water with the thermometer hanging around the freezing point, but it was better than falling into the hands of the Yankees, so of the two evils, we chose the least. My teeth chatter yet to think of that cold wade through water waist deep, covered with a thin coat of ice, but we passed it successfully, wagons and all, and then double-quicked to keep from freezing; our clothes freezing stiff on us as we came out of the water.[16]

Finally, on February 13, having been out for 11 days, and having marched all the way around the Union Army below Petersburg and back again, the weary column arrived back at their camps at Drewry's Bluff. Except for Lieutenant Lewis, every sailor and marine, every mule, and every wagon with its boat, had returned safely from the expedition.

Thus ended the Confederate Navy's last attempt to clear the James River of the enemy. "Savez" Read would go on to another adventure, this time in Louisiana, before he would be forced to lay down his sword. Some of his officers accompanied him, while others, along with many of the sailors and marines, ended the war serving with the Semmes Naval Brigade. The end would come for them in Greensboro, North Carolina, on April 28, 1865, when they were included with the surrender of General Joseph E. Johnston's Army of Tennessee. Shippey recalls, however, that upon the evacuation of Richmond in April 1865, that at least 75 members of the expedition were still in the Richmond Naval Hospital suffering from severe exposure.[17]

While the expedition was unsuccessful, it was illustrative of the audacity and courage of the men of the Confederate Navy and Marine Corps. With the return to Drewry's Bluff, Read was back in command of his one torpedo boat, the CSS *Wasp*. On the night of April 2–3, 1865, the *Wasp* would be destroyed as the last remaining Confederate troops stumbled across Mayo's Bridge on their painful trek to Appomattox.

The immense Union supply base at City Point, Virginia—Read's objective on the overland expedition

AFTERWORD

With the end of the war, the shattered relics of a small but effective Confederate Navy lay strewn across the Southern landscape. In harbors and rivers from Richmond, to Wilmington, to Charleston, to Savannah, to Mobile, to Houston, charred and twisted remains poked their rusting and rotting hulks above the surface of the waters. In addition to the remains of the once mighty ironclads, wooden gunboats, steamers, and floating and submerged mines, the occupying Union troops found numerous damaged and destroyed torpedo boats. A number of these craft had seen extensive service, while others had only recently been completed. Some were awaiting only the installation of engines and machinery in order to become operational. Exactly how many David and Squib class torpedo boats were built or nearly completed will probably never be known, but it was apparently quite a number.

Nowhere were these boats more in evidence at the end of the conflict than at Charleston. Confederate forces had evacuated the city upon the approach of General Sherman's army during the night of February 17–18, 1865, and the ironclads *Palmetto State*, *Chicora*, and *Charleston* had been blown up. Most of the surviving torpedo boats were scuttled as well, some at the wharf where they had been tied only to be left high and dry at low tide. Here their remains would be captured on film for posterity by an enterprising Northern photographer who accompanied the Union occupiers.

Chief Engineer B. E. Chassaino, USN, was one of the first Federal naval officers to explore the devastation in Charleston harbor. On March 29, he meticulously filed his reported observations with Rear Admiral Dahlgren, commander of the South Atlantic Blockading Squadron:

> In obedience to your order, I have carefully examined all the torpedo boats lying on the banks of the Cooper and Ashley Rivers, and have numbered them for convenience of reference. I submit the following report of the condition of hulls and machinery of these boats:

No. 1. Situated at the foot of Northeastern Railroad wharf. Hull in perfect condition; not entirely decked over on top, and no steering apparatus nor rudder; she lies dry at low tide and floats at high water. The boiler is complete in the boat; most parts of engine are on hand and in good condition; she needs a smokestack and line shafting.

No. 2. Situated at Northeastern Railroad wharf. Length outside, 50 feet; breadth of beam, 5½ feet (same as above). Hull in perfect condition and nearly complete, with exception of hatches. No machinery in this boat, but we have an engine without boiler which will answer the purpose.

No. 3. Situated near Chisolm's Mills. Fifty feet long; 5½ feet beam. Is sunk, but dry at low tide. Hull very imperfect, much worm-eaten, and unsound; has a large hole cut in port side and on top, aft. Is plated with one-fourth inch iron, and has a portion of torpedo apparatus attached. Boiler in bad condition; parts of engine removed and stack gone. Engine greatly corroded and worn; propeller attached; 3 feet 6 inches diameter, 20 inches face of blades, and about 15 feet pitch.

No. 4. Situated near Chisolm's Mills. Fifty feet long; 5½ feet beam. Is sunk, but dry at low tide. Hull much worm-eaten and cut up on top in vicinity of engine and boiler; a part of torpedo apparatus attached. Engine pulled to pieces and much corroded. One fan of propeller gone; smokestack in place, but in bad condition. Boilers in bad condition and pieces of machinery missing.

No. 5. Situated near Chisolm's Mills. Length, 50 feet; 6 feet beam. Hull complete; lower part much worm eaten and unsound; is plated with one-fourth inch iron. Engine and boiler passably good and nearly complete. Smokestack gone; propeller attached.

No. 6. Situated near Bennat's sawmill, west side of city. One hundred and sixty feet long, 11 feet 7 inches beam. Hull in sound condition and nearly complete externally. Boiler in place; also portion of engine. All these are in excellent condition; nearly the entire engine is on hand and is now being fitted in place.[1]

Two of the Charleston torpedo boats were towed north as trophies of war. One boat, labeled the CSS *Midge*, was placed on display at the Brooklyn Navy Yard. Unfortunately, this boat was broken up for scrap in 1877. Another boat was taken to the Naval Academy at Annapolis and put on display in the academy's museum, but the final disposition of this priceless Confederate relic is unknown today. The *Viper*, too, was captured and towed down the Chattahoochee River to Apalachicola, Florida, where she was in turn taken in tow by the USS *Yucca*. Canvas was placed over her cockpit and hatches were battened down in preparation for a tow to Key West, and then on to Norfolk. Early on May 25, 1865, the *Yucca* departed Apalachicola with the Confederate torpedo boat in tow. A few hours out into the Gulf a severe storm arose and the *Viper* began taking on large amounts of water,

A David class torpedo boat lying high and dry at low tide after the war at Charleston. Note the armor plate aft and the hole blown in the side just forward of the cuddyhole.

Naval Historical Center

A poor quality photograph of another David, lying in the mud at Charleston

Naval Historical Center

An extremely long and streamlined hull of an unfinished David torpedo boat at Charleston

Naval Historical Center

Another unfinished torpedo boat at Charleston
Portsmouth Naval Shipyard Museum

and at 2:30 p.m., the Union watch that had been placed on board was transferred to the *Yucca*. Strenuous efforts were made to keep the torpedo boat afloat, but at 4:15 p.m. the next day the towline parted and the *Viper* disappeared beneath the waves.[2]

Consequently, with the destruction of the *Midge*, the disappearance of the boat at Annapolis, and the loss of the *Viper*, no examples of Confederate torpedo boats survive today. This is unfortunate for the famous American, British, German, and Italian motor torpedo boats of two world wars in a later century owe their heritage to the David and Squib class boats of the Confederacy.

With the war over and the dream of an independent Confederate nation crushed by Northern forces, the adherents of the Confederate torpedo boats, like other disenfranchised Southerners, struggled to get on with their lives.

Matthew Fontaine Maury, the internationally acclaimed inventor and oceanographer and the first to launch torpedoes against the enemy, set sail from England on May 2, 1865, bound for Galveston, Texas. Stashed below in the blockade runner was $40,000 worth of his latest electrically detonated torpedo devices. Twenty days after departure the blockade runner put into Havana, Cuba, where Maury learned that Confederate cause had failed and the war was over. Rather than surrender and face possible prosecution by Federal authorities, he offered his services to Emperor Maximilian of Mexico where he served in the Office of the Imperial Administration of the Admiralty for a short period. In July of 1868, he finally returned to Virginia and was appointed a professor of physics at the Virginia Military Institute, a position which he held until his death on February 1, 1873.[3]

The CSS *Midge*, a David class torpedo boat on display at the Brooklyn Navy Yard after the war

Naval Historical Center

Late in 1864, Hunter Davidson, former commander of the CSS *Squib*, was dispatched to Europe to assist in the preparation of a French-built iron-clad for the Confederate Navy. February 6, 1865, found him off the coast of Spain in command of the blockade runner *City of Richmond*. Steaming laboriously beside him was the recently commissioned CSS *Stonewall* which was having difficulty negotiating the stormy winter seas. Davidson's orders were to convoy the *Stonewall* across the Atlantic where she was expected to raise great havoc among the Union blockaders. Captain Thomas J. Page of the *Stonewall*, however, instructed Davidson to leave him and go on ahead as the supplies in the hold of the *City of Richmond* were badly needed by Lee's troops around Petersburg. Davidson complied, and hoping to make Bermuda by February 15, his speedy steamer pulled away into the blinding spray of the Atlantic storm.[4]

When the battered *City of Richmond* arrived at Bermuda, Davidson learned that the last open port accessible from the island, Wilmington, North Carolina, had been closed the previous month by the capture of Fort Fisher. The final disposition of the *City of Richmond* is unknown, but it is probable that Davidson returned her to England, for in January of 1866 he signed a contract in London to purchase, equip, and provide a crew for the Chilean warship *Henrietta*.

Chile, Bolivia, Ecuador, and Peru, in a dispute with Spain, had formed an alliance to defend themselves against a threatened Spanish invasion. Much like the former Confederacy, the South American countries were desperate for warships, along with competent and experienced officers to command them. Davidson's contract called for him to attack the Spanish fleet utilizing three steam-driven torpedo boats carried on board, and, hopefully, drive the enemy from the coasts of Chile and Peru. Near the beginning of July 1866, the *Henrietta*, a fast iron-hulled steamer, left England bound for Valparaiso, Chile. When Davidson arrived on the 24th, he found, much to his disappointment, that the Spanish warships had departed three months earlier.[5]

Unwilling to return home, Davidson served the navies of at least two other governments in South America: Argentina and Venezuela. During the remaining years of his life Davidson engaged in a bitter feud with Jefferson Davis whom he contended did not give him nor the Torpedo Service proper credit in the former president's account of the American struggle. Although he did finally visit the United States several times, Davidson settled in Paraguay where he died in 1913.[6]

When the war ended, Francis D. Lee, the inventor and champion of the spar torpedo and the father of the speedy PT boats of the twentieth century, travelled to France at the invitation of Emperor Napoleon III. The fame and reputation of Lee's torpedo boats had attracted the attention of the emperor, and he was interested in having a number of the small boats built for the French Navy. After several meetings the two men could not come to an agreement, and Lee departed France, crossing the Channel to

England. There, he met with the British admiralty which was also interested in a possible torpedo fleet, but here, too, the former Confederate was
evidently unwilling to agree to their terms.

Returning to the United States, Lee settled in St. Louis and resumed
his original profession as an architect. According to his obituary, which
was printed in a Charleston newspaper, he "soon rose to the foremost rank
of his profession. His house," the article continued, "became the headquarters for all South Carolinians who passed through that city, and those who
have once been entertained by him can never forget his grand hospitality."
Several of his buildings are still in use today. In August of 1885, Lee suffered a stroke and died at the age of 58. He was laid to rest in his adopted
city of St. Louis.[7]

After surrendering with the Army of Tennessee at Greensboro, North
Carolina, on April 26, 1865, Captain Lee's immediate superior, General
Pierre G. T. Beauregard headed for his home in New Orleans, Louisiana. It
had been a frustrating war for the proud Creole general. At odds many
times with the Confederate administration over the conduct of the war,
and even of his own performance in the field, the staunch Beauregard had
displayed his finest hour in the defense of Charleston. Rising to the challenge, he had established a ring of defensive positions that a determined
but frustrated foe had found impossible to subdue. While he held the lum-
bering ironclads of Captain Tucker's Charleston Squadron in some dis-
dain, he forever championed the effectiveness and deterrent value of the
small swift torpedo boats. All of this, however, in the spring of 1865, was
now behind him.

Unlike many of his Confederate contemporaries, Beauregard fared
reasonably well after the war. Late in 1865, he was appointed superintendent of the New Orleans, Jackson, & Great Northern Railroad. The following year he also served as president of the New Orleans and Carrollton
Street Railway, a position he held for 10 years. In 1877, Beauregard, along
with former general Jubal Early, began a long tenure as supervisor of the
drawings of the infamous Louisiana Lottery, a position from which both
men reportedly received handsome salaries. In 1879, Beauregard was appointed adjutant general and commander of the Louisiana militia, a rank
he held until 1888, when he was elected commissioner of public works for
the city of New Orleans.

Unfortunately, during this time he conducted an unflattering running argument, much of it in the public press, with several of his wartime
colleagues over events at Manassas and Shiloh where he had commanded.
In a series of conflicting reminiscences the proud, old general revealed that
he disagreed with former President Jefferson Davis on just about everything. The strain of war and advancing years finally caught up with the
proud warrior, and after a short illness he passed away on February 21,
1893, at the age of 75. He was interned in the New Orleans tomb of the
Army of Tennessee in Metairie Cemetery.[8]

William T. Glassell, the first commander of the CSS *David*, spent a long term in Fort Warren, Boston, as a prisoner of war after the attack on the *New Ironsides*. He was finally exchanged at Cox's Wharf, Virginia, on October 18, 1864, and served thereafter on the ironclad *Fredericksburg* of the James River Squadron. He joined the Semmes Naval Brigade upon the evacuation of Richmond in April of 1865, and surrendered with that unit at Greensboro on April 26.

After the war Glassell was offered a position in the Peruvian Navy at the invitation of his former commander, John H. Tucker, who had emigrated from the United States to the South American country after the war. He declined the appointment and traveled to California by stagecoach accompanied by his sister and blind 74-year-old father. There, Glassell became active in real estate, becoming tract agent for his brother, Andrew, a prominent California attorney. In 1871, William laid out a town site which is known today as Orange, California. His health was not good, however, for it appears that he contracted tuberculosis during his long stay in Northern prison camps, and in 1875 the *David's* former commander moved to Los Angeles in hopes of improving his health. He died there on January 28, 1879, at the age of 48.[9]

The man who succeeded Glassell as commander of the CSS *David* and returned her safely to port on that harrowing night in 1863, James H. Tomb, was finally paroled at the end of the war at Tallahassee, Florida, on May 16, 1865. He accepted an invitation from Emperor Pedro II of Brazil to join the Brazilian Navy. Brazil at the time had united with Argentina and Uruguay in the Triple Alliance to defend themselves against the attempted military conquests of neighboring Paraguay. Tomb became the leading torpedo boat expert on the staff of the Brazilian admiral in command of the squadron operating against Paraguay. He served six years in the Brazilian Navy.

Returning to the United States in 1872, Tomb settled in St. Louis and was engaged in the hotel business for almost 40 years. Proprietor of the Mona House on North Sixth Street in 1874, he also managed the Benton Hotel on Pine Street as late as 1906. For the first 11 years Tomb was a frequent guest at the home of Francis D. Lee, and one can only imagine the lively after-dinner conversations about torpedo boats and the "Late Unpleasantness." In 1909, Tomb moved to Florida where he remained for the remainder of his waning years. The former chief engineer of the Confederate Navy commenced his final voyage, when on May 25, 1929, at the age of 90, he passed away at his home in Jacksonville, Florida.[10]

With the death of Tomb the era of the Confederate torpedo boats came to an end. None of the boats survived, and the men who built and crewed them have long since gone on to their reward. But the legacy of their accomplishments, though ignored for the most part by contemporary historians, lives on today. The Confederacy proved that small, speedy attack boats operating within the shroud of darkness could strike terror and destruction within the ranks of an overpowering and more numerous foe. These lessons were duly noted by the powers of the world and were put to lethal use in the next century. But it was the Southern nation that introduced this new form of naval warfare. Many an anxious Union sailor must have lain awake in his hammock wondering if the heavy thump he just heard was a piece of driftwood or a deadly torpedo that in the next second would blow him to kingdom come.

And therein lies the major accomplishment of Confederate torpedo boats. It was not the destruction of or damage caused to enemy vessels per se that marked their greatest achievements, but instead the large deterrent factor that they presented to the invading Federal fleets. In addition, well out of proportion to their own number, immense quantities of ships and men had to be allocated just to guard against their expected attacks. One can only speculate what would have happened if the Union forces outside Charleston had attempted to force their way into the harbor in much the same manner as Farragut had done at New Orleans. Caught in the crossfire of Confederate land fortifications, afoul of obstructions and the detonation of underwater mines, attacked by the ironclads and torpedo boats of the Charleston Squadron, it is possible that the world would have witnessed the greatest defeat ever inflicted upon the United States Navy. Federal authorities understood this (although the strength of Confederate defenses was always overestimated), and as a consequence, refrained from making such rash and irresponsible decisions.

So much more, however, could have been accomplished had the Confederate Navy Department, and in particular Secretary Mallory, realized and taken advantage of the real potential of this new weapon. As many torpedo boat proponents had correctly pointed out, several of the small but deadly boats could be constructed for every one of the materials consuming ironclads. One can only imagine how much havoc 20 or 30 boats attacking simultaneously at Charleston could have caused among the Federal blockading fleet. Even half this number, reinforced by the existing ironclads, would have been a formidable force to throw at the enemy. While the potential was great, conflicting priorities and a Southern shipbuilding industry that was strained to the breaking point prevented the Confederacy from deploying such a force.

With the war lost, her land and cities in ruins, and subjected to a brutal military occupation that the history books still unabashedly refer to as "Reconstruction," the words of General Beauregard quoted earlier echo even more clearly down through the mists of time:

> Indeed, a few years hence, we will ask ourselves in astonishment, how it was that with such a great discovery, offering such magnificent results, we never applied it to any useful purpose in this contest for our homes and independence.[11]

A David, which appears in excellent condition, afloat at the U.S. Naval Academy, Annapolis, Maryland, after the war. This boat was later put on display in the academy's museum.

Naval Historical Center

Ashore, but barely visible behind the display of naval guns in the ordnance park at the U.S. Naval Academy, is the same torpedo boat from the previous page. A new armory building was built on this site late in 1865, and the final disposition of this boat is still unknown today.

U.S. Naval Academy Museum

PPENDIX A

Southern Historical Society Papers
Volume IV
1877
Pages 225–235

REMINISCENCES OF TORPEDO SERVICE IN CHARLESTON HARBOR
by
William T. Glassell,
Commander, Confederate States Navy.

I had served, I believe faithfully, as a lieutenant in the United States navy, and had returned from China on the United States steamer "Hartford" to Philadelphia, some time in 1862, after the battles of Manassas and Ball's Bluff had been fought. I was informed that I must now take a new oath of allegiance or be sent immediately to Fort Warren. I refused to take this oath, on the ground that it was inconsistent with one I had already taken to support the Constitution of the United States. I was kept in Fort Warren about eight months, and then exchanged as a prisoner of war, on the banks of the James river. Being actually placed in the ranks of the Confederate States, I should think that even Mr. President Hayes would now acknowledge that it was my right, if not my duty, to act the part of a belligerent.

A lieutenant's commission in the Confederate States Navy was conferred on me, with orders to report for duty on the iron-clad "Chicora" at Charleston. My duties were those of a deck officer, and I had charge of the first division.

On the occasion of the attack upon the blockading squadron (making the attack at night), if I could have had any influence, we should not have fired a gun, but trusted to the effect of iron rams at full speed. It was thought, though, by older and perhaps wiser officers, that this would have been at the risk of sinking our ironclads together with the vessels of the enemy. I have ever believed there was no such danger to be apprehended; and if there was, we had better have encountered it, than to have made the fruitless attempt which we did, only frightening the enemy and putting them on their guard for the future.

It was my part, on that memorable morning, to aim and fire one effective shell into the "Keystone State" while running down to attack us, which (according to Captain LeRoy's report), killing twenty-one men and severely wounding fifteen, caused him to haul down his flag in token of surrender.

The enemy now kept at a respectful distance while preparing their iron-clad vessels to sail up more closely. Our Navy Department continued slowly to construct more of these rams, all on the same general plan, fit for little else than harbor defence. The resources of the United States being such that they could build ten iron-clads to our one, and of a superior class almost invulnerable to shot or shell, I had but little faith in the measures we were taking for defence.

Mr. Frank Lee, of the Engineers, was employed constructing torpedoes to be placed in the harbor, and called my attention to the subject. It appeared to me that this might be made an effective weapon to use offensively against the powerful vessels now being built. An old hulk was secured and Major Lee made the first experiment, as follows: A torpedo made of copper, and containing thirty or forty pounds of gunpowder, having a sensitive fuze, was attached by means of a socket to a long pine pole. To this weights were attached, and it was suspended horizontally beneath a row-boat, by cords from the bow and stern, the torpedo projecting eight or ten feet ahead of the boat, and six or seven feet below the surface. The boat was then drawn towards the hulk till the torpedo came in contact with it and exploded. The result was the immediate destruction of the old vessel and no damage to the boat.

I was now convinced that powerful engines of war could be brought into play against iron-clad ships. I believed it should be our policy to take immediate steps for the construction of a large number of small boats suitable for torpedo service, and make simultaneous attacks, if possible, before the enemy should know what we were about. The result of this experiment was represented to Commodore Ingraham. I offered all the arguments I could in favor of my pet hobby. Forty boats with small engines for this service, carrying a shield of boiler-iron to protect a man at the helm from rifle-balls, might have been constructed secretly at one-half the cost of a clumsy iron-clad. The Commodore did not believe in what he called "newfangled notions." I retired from his presence with a feeling of grief, and almost desperation, but resolved to prove at least that I was in earnest. I got row-boats from my friend, Mr. George A. Trenholm, and at his expense equipped them with torpedoes for a practical experiment against the blockading vessels at anchor off the bar.

Commodore Ingraham then refused to let me have the officers or men who had volunteered for the expedition, saying that my rank and age did not entitle me to command more than one boat. I was allowed, some time after this, to go out alone with one of these boats and a crew of six men, to attack the United States ship "Powhatan" with a fifty-pound torpedo of rifle-powder attached to the end of a long pole, suspended by wires from the bow and stern, beneath the keel of the boat, and projecting eight or ten feet ahead, and seven feet below the surface.

I started out with ebb-tide in search of a victim. I approached the ship about 1 o'clock. The young moon had gone down, and every thing seemed favorable, the stars shining over head and sea smooth and calm. The bow of the ship was towards us and the ebb-tide still running out. I did not expect to reach the vessel without being discovered, but my intention was, no matter what they might say or do, not to be stopped until our torpedo came in contact with the ship. My men were instructed accordingly. I did hope the enemy would not be alarmed by the approach of such a small boat so far out at sea, and that we should be ordered to come alongside. In this I was disappointed. When they discovered us, two or three hundred yards distant from the port bow, we were hailed and immediately ordered to stop and not come nearer. To their question, "What boat is that?" and numerous others, I gave evasive and stupid answers; and notwithstanding repeated orders to stop, and threats to fire on us, I told them I was coming on board as fast as I could, and whispered to my men to pull with all their might. I trusted they would be too merciful to fire on such a stupid set of idiots as they must have taken us to be.

My men did pull splendidly, and I was aiming to strike the enemy on the port-side, just below the gangway. They continued to threaten and to order us to lay in our oars; but I had no idea of doing so, as we were now within forty feet of the intended victim. I felt confident of success, when one of my trusted men, from terror or treason, suddenly backed his oar and stopped the boat's headway. This caused the others to give up apparently in despair. In this condition we drifted with the tide past the ship's stern, while the officer of the deck, continuing to ply me with embarrassing questions, gave orders to lower a ship's boat to go for us.

The man who backed his oar had now thrown his pistol over-board, and reached to get that of the man next to him for the same purpose. A number of men, by this time, were on deck with rifles in hand. The torpedo was now an encumbrance to retard the movements of my boat.

I never was rash, or disposed to risk my life, or that of others, without large compensation from the enemy. But to surrender thus would not do. Resolving not to be taken alive till somebody at least should be hurt, I drew a revolver and whispered to the men at the bow and stern to cut loose the torpedo.

This being quickly done, they were directed quietly to get the oars in position and pull away with all their strength. They did so. I expected a parting volley from the deck of the ship, and judging from the speed with which the little boat traveled, you would have thought we were trying to outrun the bullets which might follow us. No shot was fired. I am not certain whether their boat pursued us or not. We were soon out of sight and beyond their reach; and I suppose the captain and officers of the "Powhatan" never have known how near they came to having the honor of being the first ship ever blown up a by a torpedo boat.

I do not think this failure was from any or want of proper precaution of mine. The man who backed his oar and stopped the boat at the critical moment declared afterwards that he had been terrified so that he knew not what he was doing. He seemed to be ashamed of his conduct, and wished to go with me into any danger. His name was James Murphy, and he afterwards deserted to the enemy by swimming off to a vessel at anchor in the Edisto River.

I think the enemy must have received some hint from spies, creating a suspicion of torpedoes, before I made this attempt. I got back to Charleston after daylight next morning, with only the loss of one torpedo, and convinced that steam was the only reliable motive power.

Commodore Tucker having been ordered to command the naval forces at Charleston, torpedoes were fitted to the bows of iron-clad rams for use should the monitors enter the harbor.

My esteemed friend, Mr. Theodore Stoney, of Charleston, took measures for the construction of the little cigar-boat "David" at private express; and about this time I was ordered off to Wilmington as executive officer to attend to the equipment of the ironclad "North Carolina." She drew so much water it would have been impossible to get her over the bar, and consequently was only fit for harbor defence.

In the meantime, the United States fleet, monitors and "Ironside," crossed the bar at Charleston and took their comfortable positions protecting the army on Morris Island, and occasionally bombarding Fort Sumter.

The "North Carolina" being finished, was anchored near Fort Fisher. No formidable enemy was in sight, except the United States steamer "Minnesota," and she knowing that we could not get out, had taken a safe position at anchor beyond the bar to guard one entrance to the harbor. I made up my mind to destroy that ship or make a small sacrifice in the attempt. Accordingly, I set to work with all possible dispatch, preparing a little steam tug which had been placed under my control, with the intention of making an effort. I fitted a torpedo to her bow so that it could be lowered in the water or elevated at discretion.

I had selected eight or ten volunteers for this service, and would have taken with me one row-boat to save life in case of accident. My intention was to slip out after dark through the passage used by blockade-runners, and then to approach the big ship from seaward as suddenly and silently as possible on a dark night, making such answer to their hail and question as occasion might require, and perhaps burning a blue light for their benefit, but never stopping till my torpedo came in contact and my business was made known.

I had every thing ready for the experiment, and only waited for a suitable night, when orders came requiring me to take all the men from the "North Carolina" by railroad to Charleston immediately. An attack on that city was expected. I lost no time in obeying the order, and was informed, on arriving there, "my men were required to reinforce the crews of the gun-boats, but there was nothing in particular for me to do." In a few days, however, Mr. Theodore Stoney informed me that the little cigar boat, built at his expense, had been brought down by railroad, and that if I could do anything with her he would place her at my disposal. On examination, I determined to make a trial. She was yet in an unfinished state. Assistant-Engineer J. H. Tomb volunteered his service, and all the necessary machinery was soon fitted and got in working order, while Major Frank Lee gave me his zealous aid in fitting on a torpedo. James Stuart (alias Sullivan) volunteered to go as firemen, and afterwards the service of J. W. Cannon as pilot were secured. The boat was ballasted so as to float deeply in the water, and all above painted the most invisible color, (bluish.) The torpedo was made of copper, containing about on hundred pounds of rifle powder, and provided with four sensitive tubes of lead, containing explosive mixture; and this was carried by means of a hollow iron shaft projecting about fourteen feet ahead of the boat, and six or seven feet below the surface. I had also an armament on deck of four double-barrel shot guns, and as many navy revolvers; also, four cork life-preservers had been thrown on board, and made us feel safe.

Having tried the speed of my boat, and found it satisfactory, (six or seven knots an hour,) I got a necessary order from Commodore Tucker to attack the enemy at discretion, and also one from General Beauregard. And now came an order from Richmond, that I should proceed immediately back to rejoin the "North Carolina," at Wilmington. This was too much! I never obeyed that order, but left Commodore Tucker to make my excuses to the Navy Department.

The 5th of October, 1863, a little after dark, we left Charleston wharf, and proceeded with the ebb-tide down the harbor. A light north wind was blowing, and the night was slightly hazy, but starlight, and the water was smooth. I desired to make the attack about the turn of the tide, and this ought to have been just after nine o'clock, but the north wind made it run out a little longer.

We passed Fort Sumter and beyond the line of picket-boats without being discovered. Silently steaming along just inside the bar, I had a good opportunity to reconnoiter the whole fleet of the enemy at anchor between me and the camp-fires on Morris' Island. Perhaps I was mistaken, but it did occur to me that if we had then, instead of only one, just ten or twelve torpedoes, to make a simultaneous attack on all the ironclads, and this quickly followed by the egress of our rams, not only might this grand fleet have been destroyed, but the 20,000 troops on Morris Island been left at our mercy. Quietly maneuvering and observing the enemy, I was half an hour more waiting on time and tide. The music of drum and fife had just ceased, and the nine o'clock gun had been fired from the admiral's ship, as a signal for all unnecessary lights to be extinguished and for the men not on watch to retire for sleep. I thought the proper time for attack had arrived.

The admiral's ship, "New Ironsides," (the most powerful vessel in the world,) lay in the midst of the fleet, her starboard side presented to my view. I determined to pay her the highest compliment. I had been informed, through prisoners lately captured from the fleet, that they were expecting an attack from torpedo boats, and were prepared for it. I could, therefore, hardly expect to accomplish my object without encountering some danger from riflemen, and perhaps a discharge of grape or canister from the how-itzers. My guns were loaded with buckshot. I knew that if the officer of the deck could be disabled to begin with, it would cause them some confusion and increase our chance for escape, so I determined that if the occasion offered, I would commence by firing the first shot. Accordingly, having on a full head of steam, I took charge of the helm, it being so arranged that I could sit on deck and work the wheel with my feet. Then directing the engineer and firemen to keep below and give me all the speed possible, I gave a double-barrel gun to the pilot, with instructions not to fire until I should do so, and steered directly for the monitor. I intended to strike her just under the gang-way, but the tide still running out, carried us to a point nearer the quarter. Thus we rapidly approached the enemy.

When within about 300 yards of her a sentinel hailed us: "Boat ahoy! boat ahoy!" repeating the hail several times very rapidly. We were coming towards them with all speed, and I made no answer, but cocked both bar-rels of my gun. The officer of the deck next made his appearance, and loudly demanded, "What boat is that?" Being now within forty yards of the ship, and plenty of headway to carry us on, I thought it about time the fight should commence, and fired my gun. The officer of the deck fell back mor-tally wounded (poor fellow), and I ordered the engine stopped. The next moment the torpedo struck the vessel and exploded. What amount of di-rected damage the enemy received I will not attempt to say. My little boat plunged violently, and a large body of water which had been thrown up descended upon her deck, and down the smoke-stack and hatchway.

I immediately gave orders to reverse the engine and back off. Mr. Tomb informed me then that the fires were put out, and something had become jammed in the machinery so that it would not move. What could be done in this situation? In the mean time, the enemy recovering from the shock, beat to quarters, and general alarm spread through the fleet. I told my men I thought our only chance to escape was by swimming, and I think

I told Mr. Tomb to cut the water-pipes, and let the boat sink. Then taking one of the cork floats, I got into the water and swam off as fast as I could.

The enemy, in no amiable mood, poured down upon the bubbling water a hailstorm of rifle and pistol shots from the deck of the "Ironsides," and from the nearest monitor. Sometimes they struck very close to my head, but swimming for life, I soon disappeared from their sight, and found myself all alone in the water. I hoped that, with the assistance of flood-tide, I might be able to reach Fort Sumter, but a north wind was against me, and after I had been in the water more than an hour, I became numb with cold, and was nearly exhausted. Just then the boat of a transport schooner picked me up, and found, to their surprise, that they had captured a rebel.

The captain of this schooner made me as comfortable as possible that night with whiskey and blankets, for which I sincerely thanked him. I was handed over next morning to the mercy of Admiral Dahlgren. He ordered me to be transferred to the guard-ship "Ottowa," lying outside the rest of the fleet. Upon reaching the quarter-deck of this vessel, I was met and recognized by her Commander, William D. Whiting. He was an honorable gentleman and high-toned officer. I was informed that his orders were to have me put in irons, and if obstreperous, in double irons. I smiled, and told him his duty was to obey orders, and mine to adapt myself to circumstances. I could see no occasion to be obstreperous.

I think Captain Whiting, felt mortified at being obliged thus to treat an old brother officer, whom he knew could only have been actuated by a sense of patriotic duty in making the attack which caused him to fall into his power as a prisoner of war. At any rate, he proceeded immediately to see the admiral, and upon his return I was released, on giving my parole not to attempt an escape from the vessel. His kindness, and the gentlemanly courtesy with which I was treated by other officers of the old navy, I shall ever remember most gratefully. I learned that my fireman had been found hanging on to the rudder-chains of the "Ironsides" and taken on board. I had every reason to believe that the other two, Mr. Tomb and Mr. Cannon, had been shot or drowned, until I heard of their safe arrival in Charleston.

I was retained as a prisoner in Fort La Fayette and Fort Warren for more than a year, and learned while there that I had been promoted for what was called "gallant and meritorious service."

What all the consequences of this torpedo attack upon the enemy were is not for me to say. It certainly awakened them to a sense of the dangers to which they had been exposed, and caused them to apprehend far greater difficulties and dangers than really existed should they attempt to enter the harbor with their fleet. It may have prevented Admiral Dahlgren from carrying out the intention he is said to have had of going in with twelve ironclads on the arrival of his double-turreted monitor to destroy the city by a cross-fire from the two rivers. It certainly caused them to take many precautionary measures for protecting their vessels which had never before been thought of. Possibly it shook the nerve of a brave admiral and deprived him of the glory of laying low the city of Charleston. It was said, by officers of the navy, that the ironclad vessels of that fleet were immediately enveloped like women in hoop-skirt petticoats of netting, to lay in idle admiration of themselves for many months. The "Ironsides" went into dry-dock for repairs.

The attack also suggested to officers of the United States Navy that this was a game which both sides could play at, and Lieutenant Cushing bravely availed himself of it. I congratulate him for the *eclat* and promotion he obtained thereby. I do not remember the date of my exchange again as a prisoner of war, but it was only in time to witness the painful agonies and downfall of an exhausted people, and the surrender of a hopeless cause.

I was authorized to equip and command any number of torpedo boats, but it was now too late. I made efforts to do what I could at Charleston, till it became necessary to abandon that city. I then commanded the ironclad "Fredericksburg" on the James River, until ordered by Admiral Semmes to burn and blow her up when Richmond was evacuated. Leaving Richmond with the admiral, we now organized the First Naval Artillery Brigade, and I was in command of a regiment of sailors when informed that our noble old General, R. E. Lee, had capitulated. Our struggle was ended.

All that is now passed, and our duty remains to meet the necessities of the future. After the close of the war I was offered a command and high rank under a foreign flag. I declined the compliment and recommended my gallant old commander, Commodore J. R. Tucker, as one more worthy and competent than myself to fill a high position.

In conclusion let me say: I have never regretted that I acted in accordance with what appeared to be my duty. I was actuated by no motive of self-interest, and never entertained a feeling of hatred or personal enmity against those who were my honorable opponents. I have asked for no pardon, which might imply an acknowledgment that I had been either traitor or rebel. No amnesty has been extended to me.

Bear in mind, loyal reader, these facts: I had been absent nearly two years. No one could have lamented the beginning of the war more than I did. It had been in progress nearly six months when I came home from sea. I had taken no part in it, when on my arrival in Philadelphia, only because I could not truthfully swear that I felt no human sympathy for my own family and for the friends of my childhood, and that I was willing to shed their blood and desolate their homes; and because I would not take an oath that would have been a lie, I was denounced as a traitor, thrown into prison for eight months, and then exchanged as a prisoner of war.

I may have been a fool. I supposed or believed that the people of the south would never be conquered. I hardly hoped to live through the war. Though I had no intention of throwing my life away, I was willing to sacrifice it, if necessary, for the interests of a cause I believed to be just. I was more regardless of my own interests and those of my family than I should have been. A large portion even of my paper salary was never drawn by me. Nearly every thing I had in the world was lost, even the commission I had received for gallant and meritorious conduct, and I possess not even a token of esteem from those for whom I fought to leave, when I die, to those I love.

But the time has arrived when I think it my duty to grant pardon to the government for all injustice and injury I have received. I sincerely hope that harmony and prosperity may yet be restored to the United States of America.

PPENDIX B

Confederate Veteran
April 1914

SUBMARINES AND TORPEDO BOATS, C.S.N.

By
James H. Tomb, Chief Engineer, CSN

The first torpedo boat to be called the "David" was built at Charleston, S. C., in 1863 by Capt. Tho. Stoney Ravennel and other merchants of that city, but was not a submarine boat in any way. At the time this boat was being constructed Lieut. W. T. Glassell, C. S. N., Maj. Francis D. Lee, Engineer Corps, C. S. A., and I, Chief Engineer C. S. N., had been experimenting with the first and second cutters of the *Chicora* with a torpedo attached to a spar projecting some ten feet from the bow and held in position seven feet below the surface by perpendicular rods at the bow and stern of the cutter. While the attachment was not just what we wanted, it did very well. The torpedo was made of copper and contained sixty-five pounds of rifle powder.

Lieutenant Glassell made three attempts with the first cutter to reach the monitors at anchor off Morris Island, and I made two in the second cutter; but in each case we had the same trouble and made the same report to Flag Officer Tucker—viz: "We could not depend upon the crew pulling with any force when within sight of the enemy, and as each trip was made on the last of the ebb tide, so as to strike on the first of flood, we made no headway when we struck it, and so we had to return without accomplishing anything."

At this time the *David* was not quite ready. Captain Stoney and others made application to Flag Officer Tucker for Lieutenant Glassell and myself to take charge of the boat and after attaching the torpedo make an attack on the United States steamship *New Ironsides*, the most powerful ship of the enemy lying off Charleston. Captain Stoney named her the *David* from the great disparity between her and the duty she had to perform in the effort to destroy the *Ironsides*.

The David was built of wood in the shape of a cigar, fifty feet long by six feet beam amidships. The boiler was forward and the engine aft. Between them was a cuddyhole for the officers and what other crew the boat might carry, which was entered by a hatchway. The hull was about half above water.

The torpedo was attached to a spar made of a three-inch boiler tube and was fixed in position before leaving the dock in Charleston, and it could be neither raised nor lowered after starting on the expedition. A two-bladed propeller drove the *David* about seven knots. The torpedo was of copper, having three tubes which contained a glass tube filled with sulphuric acid and fulminate, etc., between; the outside tube was of lead.

When ready for action the boat was so well submerged that nothing was visible except her smokestack, the hatch coamings, and frame holding the torpedo spar. Lieut. W. T. Glassell was in command. Under him were Engineer James H. Tomb, Fireman J. Sullivan, and Pilot W. Canners.

The Confederates desired very much to destroy the frigate *New Ironsides*. The night selected was October 5, 1863, about one year previous to the destruction of the *Albemarle* by Lieutenant Cushing of the United States navy. There was a mist over the harbor when the *David* started. Running down guard boats, reaching the *Ironsides* shortly before 9 p.m. As the flood tide had not yet set in, we laid off and on till 9 p.m., when it was thought best to run for the *Ironsides* before we were discovered. When within a short distance of her, and steaming about seven knots, they hailed us; but the only reply was a shot from a double-barreled gun in the hands of Lieutenant Glassell. The next moment we struck her some fifteen feet forward of the counter. The torpedo exploded, and the big frigate was shaken from stem to stern, but the explosion produced a bad effect on the *David*. The volume of water thrown up, passing down the smokestack, put out the fires and filled the body of the boat, as well as disabled the engine. Lieutenant Glassell then gave orders for each man to look out for himself, and we all went overboard. Lieutenant Glassell was picked up by a transport schooner, Sullivan by the *Ironsides*, and Canners, who could not swim, stuck to the *David*. I swam some distance down the harbor; but finding that my clothing was impeding my progress, and looking back and seeing that the *David* was still afloat, I concluded to return and try to save her. After getting aboard I adjusted the machinery, started tip the fires once more, and, helping the pilot aboard, proceeded up the harbor, turning between the *Ironsides* and a monitor to prevent them from using their heavy guns on us in passing. The *Ironsides* fired three shots from her heavy gains, which passed over us.

All this time there was a heavy fire directed on the *David* from small arms from the deck of the *Ironsides*, riddling every part of the *David* above water. As we returned up the harbor we passed through the fleet and by the guard boats without further damage to us; and rounding under the stern of the flagship, I made my report to Flag Officer Tucker with nothing on but my undershirt.

The damage to the *Ironsides* was not as serious as it would have been had the torpedo been eight feet below the surface in place of six and a half, as was intended; but finding a flaw in the tube we had for a spar, it was necessary to bring it up that much. There was some serious damage done to her hull, however, as she did not fire another shot on Charleston and was sent North later for repairs.

I was put in command of the *David* and had one-quarter inch of steel placed over the hull above the water line, a cap put over the stack to prevent water from passing down, and arranged the spar so that we could lower it to any depth from the inside or keep the torpedo above the surface.

When the *David* was ready for service, I was sent to the North Edisto to make an attack on the United States steamship *Memphis*, Engineer Tomb in charge, with Pilots Canners, and Acosta, and Fireman Lawless. A section of artillery under Captain Stoney was sent ahead to assist the *David*.

On the night of March 4, 1864, we reached a point just above the anchorage of the Memphis, whose light was plainly seen; but the feed pipe gave out, and we decided to return up the river. The next night about 11:30 p.m., when in about the position, the pump again gave out; but making fast to the marsh, we repaired the pump and proceeded on down in the direction of the *Memphis*. About 12:30 a.m. of the 6th we came within hailing distance, but paid no attention to the hail, and they began firing upon us with small arms; but the shot, striking the steel shield, passed off without doing any injury to the boat or crew. The next moment the *David* struck her on the port quarter under the counter, the engine of the *David* backing at the time. The blow was a fine one, but the torpedo failed to explode. We then made a turn to port and came back at her on the starboard side; but as the *Memphis* had been working ahead, we passed under her counter, carrying away a portion of the *David's* stack, made glancing blow, and again failed to explode the torpedo. Failing in our last attack, we decided to return to Church Flats and examine the torpedo, etc. As we steamed back up the river the *Memphis* made use of her heavy guns, but all the shot passed well over us and did no damage.

Reaching Church Flats and making an examination of the torpedo, we found that the first blow was a good one, as the tube containing the acid was mashed flat, but, being defective, had failed to explode. The other one was not a good blow, as the lead tube on the outside was bent the least bit, but the tube containing the acid was not broken. The torpedo contained five pounds of rifle powder, thirteen pounds more than we used on the *Ironsides*; and had the tube been perfect, we would have blown the whole stern from the *Memphis*.

The *David* returned to Charleston, and while on duty, passing out beyond Fort Sumter at night, did not make another attack on the blockading ships, except on one night in April, when we ran out of Charleston, intending to strike the United States steamship *Wabash*; but there was such a heavy swell that in heading for the *Wabash* the sea would roll on board the *David*, and she came so near sinking that we were compelled to return to Charleston. We headed for the *Wabash* three times.

The *David* had orders to tow the submarine torpedo boat commanded by Lieutenant Dixon past Fort Sumter whenever he wished to run out to make an attack on the blockaders, and in towing him out we came near being blown up by his torpedo getting adrift, (At this stage the CSS *H. L. Hunley* was towing its torpedo on a long line) I advised Lieutenant Dixon to use the torpedo just as it was used by the *David*, as I did not think his boat had sufficient power to back out if it was submerged, and the suction from the sinking ship would be apt to keep him under the water. Lieutenant Dixon gave me to understand that he would remain on the surface. I requested Flag Officer Tucker to relieve the *David* from the duty of towing his boat on account of the danger. That same month Lieutenant Dixon ran out of Charleston and striking the United States steamship *Housatonic*, sank her, and he was lost with all on board the torpedo boat, as she went to the bottom with the *Housatonic*.

When we think of the number of brave men who lost their lives on this ill-fated craft, it brings out the fine qualities of Lieutenant Dixon who in all this never lost confidence either in the boat or himself. There were in all thirty-three lost in her from her first appearance at Mobile to the sinking of the *Housatonic*. The army or the navy had no more gallant officer than Lieutenant Dixon, of the C. S. A.

* * * * *

The following is the official report as to the condition of the *Ironsides*, showing how serious was the damage caused by the *David*:

U. S. S. *New Ironsides*, off Morris Island, S. C.,

November 24, 1863.

Rear Admiral John A. Dahlgren, U. S. N.

Sir: In obedience to your orders, I have examined the injuries discovered in the coal bunkers resulting from the attack made on the ship by the Rebel torpedo boat *David* on the night of the 5th, and found them to be as follows: One hanging knee abreast the engine room started off ten inches from clamp and ceiling, two-stroke clamps and five-stroke earrings broken in two in a perpendicular line. The banking knee is started entirely from the beam and the beam badly smashed. The fore and aft piece that forms the engine room is split for a space of about four feet and likewise started from the ends of the spur beams from three to four inches; six of the lap knees are also started. The stanchions that support the fore and aft pieces of the engine room, and likewise form the coal bunkers, are entirely gone at the heads: the ceiling is started off from the frame of the ship for a space of ten feet both forward and aft of the hanging knee; forward of the knee where the ceiling forms a butt it has started ten inches from the ship frame, and the side of the ship is sprung in from four to five inches for a space of forty feet.

When the ship was examined by the divers outside, they reported that the planking abreast the engine room was shattered for a space of six feet in depth to ten or twelve feet in length and about one and a half inches in the face of the planking. The oakum is also started in the seams. In examining the gun and berth decks I find the spaketing and waterways on both decks started in three inches for a space of twenty feet. The bulkheads and shelving of the storerooms abreast the engine room were entirely knocked down. The stanchions that support the fore and aft pieces that form the engine room on the gun deck were carried away at the heels, carrying the joiner work with them. The stanchions that support the spar deck around the engine room were jumped out of the iron sockets by the shock.

The waterway on the gun deck abreast of the engine room is started from the deck three-quarters of an inch for a space of thirty feet, causing the deck to leak badly. The above injuries were all caused by the explosion of the torpedo.

In my opinion, this ship ought to be docked as soon as she can possibly be spared from this harbor.

Very respectfully, your obedient servant,

T. H. Bishop, Carpenter, U. S. N.

Appendix C

Southern Historical Society Papers
Volume II
1876
Pages 1–6

ELECTRICAL TORPEDOES AS A SYSTEM OF DEFENCE.
By
Hunter Davidson, Commander, CSN

New York Hotel, New York, May, 1874.

I have but recently returned from South America, and had an opportunity of reading two works on torpedoes, or submarine mines; one by Major R. H. Stotherd, R. E., and the other by Commander Fisher, R. N.

It is now nine years since the close of our civil war, and considering how rapidly things change in this fast age, and that we too must soon pass away, it is about time at least to commence to vindicate the truth of history; for much of the history of that conflict exists only in the memory of the actors therein, and if they die without recording their experiences the truth is lost.

At this day I think that my letter may be fairly read and considered, and that the impartial historian will give to my statements their due weight, the object to establish my claim to having made the first successful application torpedoes or submarine mines as a system of defence in time of war, which system is now generally adopted in some modified from by all nations for the defence of harbors, rivers, &c., and their approaches, as well as for the approaches by land to any fortified position.

I do not know that I should ever have taken this step, but that the authors of the books to which I allude, as well as Colonel Chesney, R. E., in his "Essays in Military Biography," page 345, seem to turn their backs, with such a studied air, upon the practical source of electrical torpedo defences—defences which they do not conceal are becoming the chief reliance of all nations for the purposes above named.

The works of Major Stotherd, R. E., particularly the last edition, are valuable alike to the general reader, the officer of whatever service of his country, and to the young torpedoist; whilst those of Commander Fisher are rather elementary and wanting in practical information to be sure; but both of those authors would doubtless have it inferred that to England belongs the merit, whatever it amounts, of having devised, without material assistance, an efficient a matter of any practical importance treated of by Major Stotherd in his late work on this subject, that was not understood and practiced where necessary in my torpedo department during the late war, except as to the new explosives; and I assert that he could easily have ascertained these facts by making the ordinary inquiries that every author should make in order to place before his readers a correct and impartial work; also that the facts already at his hand should have induced him to do so, for he quotes from the pamphlet on torpedo warfare, by Captain E. Harding, Steward, R. E., whose constant mention of my name in connection with the first and only success of electrical torpedoes in war, showed Major Stotherd very clearly where the system originated.

And now for the evidence. First, let me say, that I purposely avoided entering into detail, until forced to do so, as to what was done, by the use of E. torpedoes during the our civil war, not wishing to recall unpleasant scenes, but that I write now in gratification of a natural and proper ambition, recording the truth.

The first idea of using torpedoes on the Confederate side, originated I believe with the Hon. S. R. Mallory, Secretary of the Navy, and he directed the distinguished Captain M. F. Maury, LL. D., to make experiments with a view to their general employment if practicable. I was selected as his immediate assistant. His work commenced in the spring of 1862, and continued for a few months only with electrical torpedoes.

He had arrived at no definite conclusion form his experiments, in any particular when he left the Confederacy for Europe, and I was ordered to take charge, subject to orders form the Navy Department only, and remained so until near the closing scenes of the war, when I was relieved in command by Captain J. Pembroke Jones.

The means used in my electrical torpedo defences differed in every essential particular from those used by Captain Maury in his experiments. The peculiar construction of the mines, the methods of fixing them in position and connecting them with the cables and batteries; the determination of the quantities of powder to use at different depths and the effective areas, the batteries used for firing, and also for testing the mines, as well as the organization and equipment of the stations from which the mines were controlled, all formed a complete system devised by myself.

The results of this system were that the first vessels ever injured or destroyed in war, by electrical torpedoes, were by the torpedo department operating under my immediate command, and I may add the only ones, that I am aware of.

Those who are not well acquainted with the history of our civil war will find ample proof of my statements on file in the Navy Department at Washington, as also by reference to Admirals Porter and S. P. Lee, and Commander W. B. Cushing, United States Navy, for the fact that an efficient system of torpedo defences did exist on the James river, during the war, and to the Hon. S. R. Mallory; Captain J. M. Brooke, inventor of the Merrimac, the Brooke Gun, and the deep-sea sounding apparatus; and also to Captain Wm. H. Parker, formerly Superintendent of the Confederate Naval School, that I organized and commanded these defences, and was the first to make them successful. There are volumes of evidence to his effect that can be produced when necessary.

I hold letters from the three last named gentlemen, and from the late General R. E. Lee in reference to the efficiency of my torpedo department-also a letter from the Hon. S. R. Mallory, in which he says: "I regarded your service as equivalent to that of a well appointed fleet or army;" and this had reference only of the defences of Richmond. In fact when the system was nearly completed and inspected in person by President Davis, General Lee, and Secretary Mallory, it was immediately decided to withdraw large numbers of troops from that quarter for offensive operations elsewhere, it being well understood that the Union armies could not advance without the assistance of the Federal squadron, which advance was for a long time effectually prevented by my system of submarine defences.

Many vessels were disabled or destroyed by mechanical or contact torpedoes, but such effect is known to be the result of mere chance, often as fatal to friend as foe, and produces no such demoralizing effect as the certain destruction which awaits any vessel attempting to pass electrical torpedoes.

In regard to the efficiency of the torpedo defences employed by me during the war, as compared with those of the present day, I have to say that I have been almost constantly on torpedo duty ashore and afloat since our war, making the subject a study in several foreign countries and our own, and have not yet seen any material improvement or development of the original system, and if we were at war with any great naval power to-morrow, I should prefer to rely upon it when the hour of trial came.

There are several beautiful and ingenious methods devised by those who have had no practice in war, but my experience will not permit me to give them approval.

Now, if we are to consider practical success as the test of an invention, have I not a right to this? Am I not as much entitled to it as Morse of the telegraph? Howe to the sewing machine? Colt to the revolver? And as many other men to their inventions whose success did not carry with it the original conception of the necessity for the invention, nor the first attempts to carry out the idea, nor in whose inventions as patented is there one original scientific principle? It is the effect produced by art in combination, and this is the basis of ninety-nine out of a hundred patents.

And the first successful attempt to achieve an important physical object by original principles or art in combining those which are known, is the only test by which we can by governed in awarding a patent entitling one to invention. If not, where shall we draw the line of distinction? How shall we proceed with a patent office?

In the year 1860, Congress adopted by an almost unanimous vote my invention for "lowering, detaching, attaching, and securing boats at sea," and directed the Secretary of the Navy to purchase the patent right for the use of the navy, which was done. The marine world had probably seen the necessity for such an invention since the days of Noah, and there is not one original mechanical principle in it. It is simply a combination. The invention was several years before the country, in scientific journals; was carefully examined and tested at sea in several ships by some of the best officers in the navy, and discussed during two sessions in Congress, yet I have never known any one to dispute my claim thereto.

The efficiency of electrical torpedo defences is so universally recognized at this day and they appear so simple to the initiated, that many of the "I know it" kind may exclaim, "Why I don't see any invention in the matter, for it has been long known that if a chance was got at a ship with so much powder under her, she was bound go up." But then if so simple, why did not Fulton or Bushnell, in the early history of our country, or the Russians during the Crimean War, stamp the fact upon the times, so as to render it, as it is now, a system of defence that no nation dares neglect.

And how did it become so? I trust to history for the answer.

If any one had to contend with the abuse and sneers, and ridicule whilst in the performance of torpedo duty day and night, that fell upon me during the war, he would realize that as late as the summer of 1863, some of the ablest men of the day did not regard torpedo warfare as worthy of consideration, and the very attempts of Fulton and Bushnell, and of the Russians, were used by those men in argument that my attempt would also be fruitless.

Much of the light has to struggle through mediums of darkness and resistance, and gradually breaks in upon us. Our theories rarely assume a practical from, but as in many other circumstances so in naval and military matters we are controlled by theory (nearly every association having one of its own) until the test, the practice comes, and then in war see how the mist vanishes and light appears! Some have made the lucky casts and win.

Can any one think of a war that did not cause him to wonder at his own want of forethought? How weapons and methods are changed! How rank is capsized! How he came out of the struggle other rounds higher on the ladders of science and of art! And every discovery of a new or improved weapon proves to be a step towards greater civilization and peace.

Apropos of the foregoing, I remember that a distinguished Admiral sent word to me when under a flag of truce during the war, that if I came down to his squadron again in a certain boat, (in which I had made the first successful attack with the "Lee-Spar-Torpedo") he would not respect the flag, as he did not acknowledge that I was engaged in civilized or legitimate warfare. This glanced from my armor as many a worse shot did from my own side, though for other reasons, for I felt that as he was the only sufferer then, he saw the matter from but one point of view, but that time would set it even as I replied in substance to the officer, ——— "*respice finem.*" The end indeed was not far off, for the official reports of the day were that the admiral took up my torpedo mines as the territory was conquered, and turned them against us; and certain it is that his squadron was soon after armed with the "Lee-Spar-Torpedo."

To those who know me, I trust that this letter is unnecessary, but then there is the world beside, and who knows how many in it to set up a claim without having a knowledge of the facts? And those too who having that dangerous "little knowledge" may constantly employ it, as they have already done, until public opinion accepts it as its guide.

I cannot conclude without a few words more in reference to my ever kind and lamented friend Captain Maury. He went from the South to England, where he continued to make experiments in ingenious method of arranging and testing torpedo mines, which I believe is his patent, and was shown me by him in the winter of 1864 and '65.

The fact that there was no practical result from his experiments the few months he carried them on in the South, is due simply to the want of time to organize his forces and collect material, though his experiments served to mark some of the shoals on the way, if not the channel to success. But even had he remained to develop the system, and given in the greater impress of his genius, no success in consequence could have added much to the world-wide fame he had already acquired.

To the Hon. S. R. Mallory, who always believed in the success of the undertaking from the first, and ever gave me a firm and kind support, and materially aided me with his advice; to Captain Jno. M. Brooke, then Chief of the Naval Bureau of Ordnance, and to my electrical, R. O. Crowley, I am in a great measure indebted for the success which I here claim entitles me to be known as having made the first successful application of electrical torpedoes, or submarine mines in time of war, and as a system of defence.

PPENDIX D

Southern Historical Society Papers
Volume V
1878
Pages 145–155

TORPEDO SERVICE IN THE HARBOR
AND WATER DEFENSES OF CHARLESTON
By
General P. G. T. Beauregard

On my return to Charleston in September, 1862, to assume command of the Department of South Carolina and Georgia, I found the defenses of those two States in a bad and incomplete condition, including defective location and arrangement of works, even at Charleston and Savannah. Several points—such as the mouths of the Stono and Edisto rivers, and the headwaters of Broad river at Port Royal—I found unprotected; though soon after the fall of Fort Sumter, in 1861, as I was about to be detached, I had designated them to be properly fortified. A recommendation had even been made by my immediate predecessor that the outer defenses of Charleston Harbor should be given up as untenable against the ironclads and monitors then known to be under construction at the North, and that the waterline of the immediate city of Charleston should be made the sole line of defense. This course, however, not having been authorized by the Richmond authorities, it was not attempted, except that the fortifications of Cole's Island—the key to the defense of the Stono river—was abandoned and the harbor in the mouth of the Stono left open to the enemy, who made it their base of operations. Immediately on my arrival I inspected the defenses of Charleston and Savannah, and made a requisition on the War Department for additional troops and heavy guns deemed necessary; but neither could be furnished, owing, it was stated, to the pressing wants of the Confederacy at other points. Shortly afterward Florida was added to my command, but without any increase of troops or guns, except the few already in that State; and, later, several brigades were withdrawn from me, notwithstanding my protest, to reinforce the armies of Virginia and Tennessee.

As I have already said, I found at Charleston an exceedingly bad defensive condition against a determined attack. Excepting Fort Moultrie, on Sullivan's Island, the works and batteries covering Charleston Harbor, including Fort Sumter, were insufficiently armed and their barbette guns without the protection of heavy traverses. In all the harbor works there were only three 10-inch and a few 8-inch Columbiads, which had been left in Forts Sumter and Moultrie by Major Anderson, and about a dozen rifle guns—un-banded 32-pounders, made by the Confederates—which burst after a few discharges. There were, however, a number of good 42-pounders of the old pattern, which I afterward had rifled and banded. I found a continuous floating boom of large timbers bound together and interlined, stretching across from Fort Sumter to Fort Moultrie. But this was a fragile and unreliable barrier, as it offered too great a resistance to the strong current of the ebb and flood tide at full moon, especially after southeasterly gales, which backed up the waters in the bay and in the Ashley and Cooper rivers. It was exposed, therefore, at such periods, to be broken, particularly as the channel-bottom was hard and smooth, and the light anchors which held the boom in position were constantly dragging—a fact which made the breaking of the boom an easy matter under the strain of hostile steamers coming against it under full headway. For this reason the engineers had proposed the substitution of a rope obstruction, which would be free from tidal strain, but little had been done toward its preparation. I, therefore, soon after summing command, ordered its immediate completion, and, to give it protection and greater efficiency, directed that two lines of torpedoes be planted a few hundred yards in advance of it. But before the order could be carried out, a strong southerly storm broke the timber boom in several places, leaving the channel unprotected, except by the guns of Forts Sumter and Moultrie. Fortunately, however, the Federal fleet made no effort to enter the harbor, as it might have done if it had made the attempt at night. A few days later the rope obstruction and torpedoes were in position, and so remained without serious injury till the end of the war.

The rope obstruction was made of two heavy cables, about five or six feet apart, the one below the other, and connected together by a network of smaller ropes. The anchors were made fast to the lower cable, and the buoys or floats to the upper one. The upper cable carried a fringe of smaller ropes, about three-fourths of an inch in diameter by fifty feet long, which floated as so many "streamers" on the surface, destined to foul the screw propeller of any steamer which might attempt to pass over the obstruction. Shortly after these cables were in position a blockade-runner, in attempting at night to pass through the gap purposely left open near the Sullivan Island shore, under the guns of Fort Moultrie and of the outside batteries, accidentally crossed the end of the rope obstruction, when one of the streamers got entangled around the shaft, checking its revolutions. The vessel was at once compelled to drop anchor to avoid drifting on the torpedoes or ashore, and afterward had to be docked for the removal of the streamer before she could again use her propeller. The torpedoes, as anchored, floated a few feet below the surface of the water at low tide, and were loaded with one hundred pounds of powder arranged to explode by concussion—the automatic fuse employed being the invention of Capt. Francis D. Lee, an intelligent young engineer officer of my general staff, and now a prominent architect in St. Louis. The fuse or firing apparatus consisted of a cylindrical lead tube with a hemispherical head, the metal in the head being thinner than at the sides. The tube was open at the lower extremity, where it was surrounded by a flange; and, when in place, it was protected against leakage by means of brass couplings and rubber washers. It was charged as follows: In its center was a glass tube filled with sulfuric acid and hermetically sealed. This was guarded by another glass tube sealed in like manner, and both were retained in position by means of a peculiar pin at the open end of the leaden tube; the space between the latter and the glass tube was then filled with a composition of chlorate of potassa and powdered loaf sugar, with a quantity of rifle powder. The lower part of the tube was then closed with a piece of oiled paper. Great care had to be taken to ascertain that the leaden tube was perfectly water-tight under considerable pressure. The torpedo also had to undergo the most careful test. The firing of the tube was produced by bringing the thin head in contact with a hard object, as the side of a vessel; the indentation of the lead broke the glass tubes, which discharged the acid on the composition, firing it, and thereby igniting the charge in the torpedo.

The charges used varied from sixty to one hundred pounds rifle powder, though other explosives might have been more advantageously used if they had been available to us. Generally four of the fuses were attached to the head of each torpedo so as to secure the discharge at any angle of attack. These firing tubes or fuses were afterward modified to avoid the great risk consequent upon screwing them in place and of having them permanently attached to the charged torpedo. The shell of the latter was thinned at the point where the tube was attached, so that, under water pressure, the explosion of the tube would certainly break it and discharge the torpedo; though, when unsubmerged, the explosion of the tube would vent itself in the open air without breaking the shell. In this arrangement the tube was of brass, with a leaden head, and made water-tight by means of a screw plug at its base. Both the shell and the tube being made independently water-tight, the screw connection between the two was made loose, so that the tube could be attached or detached readily with the fingers. The mode adopted for testing against leakage was by placing them in a vessel of alcohol, under the glass exhaust of an air-pump. When no air bubbles appeared the tubes could be relied on. Captain Lee had also an electric torpedo which exploded by concussion against a hard object; the electric current being thus established, insured the discharge at the right moment.

Captain Lee is the inventor also of the "spar-torpedo" as an attachment to vessels, now in general use in the Federal navy. It originated as follows: He reported to me that he thought he could blow up successfully any vessel by means of a torpedo carried some five or six feet under water at the end of a pole ten or twelve feet long, which should be attached to the bow of a skiff or row-boat. I authorized an experiment upon the hulk of an unfinished and condemned gunboat anchored in the harbor, and loaded for the purpose with all kinds of rubbish taken from the "burnt district" of the city. It was a complete success; a large hole was made in the side of the hulk, the rubbish being blow high in the air, and the vessel sank in less than a minute. I then determined to employ this important invention, not only in the defense of Charleston, but to disperse or destroy the Federal blockading fleet by means of one or more small swift steamers, with low decks, and armed only with "spar-torpedoes" as designed by Captain Lee. I sent him at once to Richmond, to urge the matter on the attention of the Confederate Government. He reported his mission as follows:

"In compliance with your orders, I submitted the drawing of my torpedo and a vessel with which I propose to operate them, to the Secretary of War. While he heartily approved, he stated his inability to act in the matter, as it was a subject that appertained to the navy. He, however, introduced me and urged it to the Secretary of Navy. The Secretary of War could do nothing, and the Secretary of the Navy would not, for the reason that I was not a naval officer under his command. So I returned to Charleston without accomplishing anything. After a lapse of some months I was again sent to Richmond to represent the matter to the Government, and I carried with me the endorsement of the best officers of the navy. The result was the transfer of an unfinished hull, on the stocks at Charleston, which was designed for a gunboat—or rather floating battery, as she was not arranged for any motive power, but was intended to be anchored in position. This hull was completed by me, and a second-hand and much worn engine was obtained in Savannah and placed in her. Notwithstanding her tub-like model and the inefficiency of her engine, Captain Carlin, commanding a blockade-runner, took charge of her in an attack against the *New Ironsides*. She was furnished with a spar designed to carry three torpedoes of one hundred pounds each. The lateral spars suggested by you, Captain Carlin declined to use, as they would interfere very seriously with the movements of the vessel, which, even without them, could with the utmost difficulty stem the current. The boat was almost entirely submerged, and painted gray like the blockade runners, and, like them, made no smoke, by burning anthracite coal. The night selected for the attack was very dark, and the *New Ironsides* was not seen until quite near. Captain Carlin immediately made for her; but her side being oblique to the direction of his approach, he ordered his steersman, who was below deck, to change the course. This order was misunderstood, and, in place of going the 'bow on' as was proposed, she ran alongside of the *New Ironsides* and entangled her spar in the anchor-chain of that vessel. In attempting to back the engine hung on the center, and some delay occurred before it was pried off. During this critical period Captain Carlin, in answer to threats and inquiries, declared his boat to be the *Live Yankee*, from Port Royal, with dispatches for the admiral. This deception was not discovered until after Carlin had backed out and his vessel was lost in the darkness."

Shortly after this bold attempt of Captain Carlin, in the summer of 1863, to blow up the *New Ironsides*, Mr. Theodore Stone, Dr. Ravenel, and other gentlemen of Charleston, had built a small cigar-shaped boat, which they called the *David*. It had been specially planned and constructed to attack this much-dreaded naval Goliath, the *New Ironsides*. It was about twenty feet long, with a diameter of five feet at its middle, and was propelled by a small screw worked by a diminutive engine. As soon as ready for service, I caused it to be fitted with a "Lee spar-torpedo" charged with seventy-five pounds of powder. Commander W. T. Glassell, a brave and enterprising officer of the Confederate States Navy, took charge of it, and about eight o'clock one hazy night, on the ebb tide, with a crew of one engineer, J. H. Tomb; one fireman, James Sullivan; and a pilot, J. W. Cannon; he fearlessly set forth from Charleston on his perilous mission—the destruction of the *New Ironsides*. I may note that this ironclad steamer threw a great deal more metal, at each broadside, than all the monitors together of the fleet; her fire was delivered with more rapidity and accuracy, and she was the most effective vessel employed in the reduction of Battery Wagner.

The *David* reached the *New Ironsides* about ten o'clock p.m., striking her with a torpedo about six feet under water, but fortunately for that steamer she received the shock against one of her inner bulk-heads, which saved her from destruction. The water, however, being thrown up in large volume, half-filled her little assailant and extinguished its fires. It then drifted out to sea with the current, under a heavy grape and musketry fire from the much alarmed crew of the *New Ironsides*. Supposing the *David* disabled, Glassell and his men jumped into the sea to swim ashore; but after remaining in the water about one hour he was picked up by the boat of a Federal transport schooner, whence he was transferred to the guard ship *Ottowa*, lying outside of the rest of the fleet. He was ordered at first, by Admiral Dahlgren, to be ironed, and in case of resistance, to be double ironed; but through the intercession of his friend, Captain W. D. Whiting, commanding the *Ottawa*, he was released on giving his parole not to attempt to escape from the ship. The fireman, Sullivan, had taken refuge on the rudder of the *New Ironsides*, where he was discovered, put in irons and kept in a dark cell until sent with Glassell to New York, to be tried and hung, as reported by Northern newspapers, for using an engine of war not recognized by civilized nations. But the government of the United States has now a torpedo corps, intended specially to study and develop that important branch of the military service. After a captivity of many months in Forts Lafayette and Warren, Glassell and Sullivan were finally exchanged for the captain and a sailor of the Federal steamer *Isaac Smith*, a heavily-armed gunboat which was captured in the Stono River, with its entire crew of one hundred and thirty officers and men, by a surprise I had prepared, with field artillery only, placed in ambuscade along the river bank, and under whose fire the Federal gunners were unable to man and use their powerful guns. Captain Glassell's other two companions, Engineer Tomb and Pilot Cannon, after swimming about for a while, espied the *David* still afloat, drifting with the current; they betook themselves to it, re-lit the fires from its bull's-eye lantern, got up steam and started back for the city; they had to re-pass through the fleet and they received the fire of several of its monitors and guard-boats, fortunately without injury. With the assistance of the flood tide they returned to their point of departure, at the Atlantic wharf, about midnight, after having performed one of the most daring feats of the war. The *New Ironsides* never fired another shot after this attack upon her. She remained some time at her anchorage off Morris Island, evidently undergoing repairs; she was then towed to Port Royal, probably to fit her for her voyage to Philadelphia, where she remained until destroyed by fire after the war.

Nearly about the time of the attack upon the *New Ironsides* by the *David*, Mr. Horace L. Hunley, formerly of New Orleans, but then living in Mobile, offered me another torpedo-boat of a different description, which had been built with his private means. It was shaped like a fish, made of galvanized iron, was twenty feet long, and at the middle three and a half feet wide by five deep. From its shape it came to be known as the "fish torpedo-boat." Propelled by a screw worked from the inside by seven or eight men, it was so contrived that it could be submerged and worked under water for several hours, and to this end was provided with a fin on each side, worked also from the interior. By depressing the points of these fins the boat, when in motion, was made to descend, and by elevating them it was made to rise. Light was afforded through the means of bull's-eyes placed in the man-holes. Lieut. Payne, Confederate States Navy, having volunteered with a crew from the Confederacy Navy, to man the fish-boat for another attack upon the *New Ironsides*, it was given into their hands for that purpose. While tied to the wharf at Fort Johnston, whence it was to start under cover of night to make the attack, a steamer passing close by capsized and sunk it. Lieut. Payne, who at the time was standing in one of the man-holes, jumped out into the water, which, rushing into the two openings, drowned two men then within the body of the boat. After the recovery of the sunken boat Mr. Hunley came from Mobile, bringing with him Lieutenant Dixon, of the Alabama Volunteers, who had successfully experimented with the boat in the harbor of Mobile, and under him another naval crew volunteered to work it. As originally designed, the torpedo was to be dragged astern upon the surface of the water; the boat, approaching the broadside of the vessel to be attacked, was to dive beneath it, and, rising to the surface beyond, continue its course, thus bringing the floating torpedo against the vessel's side, when it would be discharged by a trigger contrived to go off by the contact. Lieutenant Dixon made repeated descents in the harbor of Charleston, diving under the naval receiving ship which lay at anchor there. But one day when he was absent from the city Mr. Hunley, unfortunately, wishing to handle the boat himself, made the attempt. It was readily submerged, but did not rise again to the surface, and all on board perished from asphyxiation. When the boat was discovered, raised and opened, the spectacle was indescribably ghastly; the unfortunate men were contorted into all kinds of horrible attitudes; some clutching candles, evidently endeavoring to force open the man-holes; others lying in the bottom tightly grappled together, and the blackened faces of all presented the expression of their despair and agony. After this tragedy I refused to permit the boat to be used again; but Lieutenant Dixon, a brave and determined man, having returned to Charleston, applied to me for authority to use it against the Federal steam sloop-of-war *Housatonic*, a powerful new vessel, carrying eleven guns of the largest caliber, which lay at the time in the north channel opposite Beach Inlet, materially obstructing the passage of our blockade-runners in and out. At the suggestion of my chief-of-staff, Gen. Jordan, I consented to its use for this purpose, not as a submarine machine, but in the same manner as the *David*. As the *Housatonic* was easily approached through interior channels from behind Sullivan's Island, and Lieutenant Dixon readily procured a volunteer crew, his little vessel was fitted with a Lee spar torpedo, and the expedition was undertaken. Lieutenant Dixon, acting with characteristic coolness and resolution, struck and sunk the *Housatonic* on the night of February 17, 1864; but unhappily, from some unknown cause, the torpedo boat was also sunk, and all with it lost. Several years since a "diver," examining the wreck of the *Housatonic*, discovered the fish-boat lying alongside of its victim.

From the commencement of the siege of Charleston I had been decidedly of the opinion that the most effective as well as least costly method of defense against the powerful iron-clad steamers and monitors originated during the late war, was to use against them small but swift steamers of light draught, very low decks, and hulls iron-claded down several feet below the water-line; these boats to be armed with a spar-torpedo (on Captain Lee's plan), to thrust out from the bow at the moment of collision, being inclined to strike below the enemy's armor, and so arranged that the torpedo could be immediately renewed from within for another attack; all

such boats to be painted gray like the blockade-runners, and, when employed, to burn anthracite coal, so as to make no smoke. But unfortunately,
I had not the means to put the system into execution. Soon after the first
torpedo attack, made, as related, by the *David* upon the *New Ironsides*, I
caused a number of boats and barges to be armed with spar-torpedoes for
the purpose of attacking in detail the enemy's gunboats resorting to the
sounds and harbors along the South Carolina coast. But, the Federals having become very watchful, surrounded their steamers at night with nettings
and floating booms to prevent the torpedo boats from coming near enough
to do them any injury. Even in the outer harbor of Charleston, where the
blockaders and their consorts were at anchor, the same precaution was
observed in clam weather.

The anchoring of the large torpedoes in position was attended with
considerable danger. While planting them at the mouth of the Cooper and
Ashley rivers (which form the peninsula of the city of Charleston), the
steamer engaged in that duty being swung around by the returning tide,
struck and exploded one of the torpedoes just anchored. The steamer sank
immediately, but, fortunately, the tide being low and the depth of water
not great, no lives were lost. In 1863-4, Jacksonville, Florida, having been
evacuated by the Confederates, then too weak to hold it longer, the Federal
gunboats frequently ran up the St. John's river many miles, committing
depredations along its banks. To stop these proceedings I sent a party from
Charleston under a staff officer, Captain Pliny Bryan, to plant torpedoes in
the channels of that stream. The result was the destruction of several large
steamers and cessation of all annoyance on the part of the others. In the bay
of Charleston and adjacent streams I had planted about one hundred and
twenty-five torpedoes and some fifty more in other parts of my department. The first torpedoes used in the late war were placed in the James
river, below Richmond, by General G. R. Raines, who became afterward
chief of the Torpedo Bureau. Mr. Barbarin, of New Orleans, placed also
successfully a large number of torpedoes in Mobile bay and its vicinity.

To show the important results obtained by the use of torpedoes by
the Confederates and the importance attached, now, at the North to that
mode of warfare, I will quote here the following remarks from an able article in the last September number of the Galaxy, entitled, "Has the Day of
Great Navies Past?" The author says: "The real application of submarine
warfare dates from the efforts of the Confederates during the late war. In
October, 1862, a 'torpedo bureau' was established at Richmond, which made
rapid progress in the construction and operations of these weapons until
the close of the war in 1865. Seven Union ironclads, eleven wooden war
vessels, and six army transports were destroyed by Southern torpedoes, and
many more were seriously damaged. This destruction occurred, for the most
part, during the last two years of the war, and it is suggestive to think
what might have been the influence on the Union cause if the Confederate

practice of submarine warfare had been nearly as efficient at the commencement as it was at the close of the war. It is not too much to say, respecting the blockade of the Southern ports, that if not altogether broken up, it would have been rendered so inefficient as to have command no respect from European powers, while the command of rivers, all important to the Union forces as bases of operations, would have been next to impossible."

"Think of the destruction this infernal machine effected, and bear in mind its use came to be fairly understood, and some system introduced into its arrangement, only during the last part of the war. During a period when scarcely any vessels were lost, and very few severely damaged by the most powerful guns then employed in actual war, we find this long list of disasters from the use of this new and, in the beginning, much despised comer into the arena of naval warfare. But it required just such a record as this to arouse naval officers to ask themselves the question, 'Is not the day of great navies gone forever?' If such comparatively rude and improvised torpedoes made use of by the Confederates caused such damage and spread such terror among the Union fleet, what will be the consequence when skillful engineers, encouraged by governments, as they have never been before, diligently apply themselves to the perfecting of this terrible weapon? The successes of Confederates have made the torpedo, which before was looked on with loathing—a name not to be spoken except contemptuously—a recognized factor in modern naval warfare. On all sides we see the greatest activity in improving it."

I shall now refer briefly to the use in Charleston harbor of rifle-cannon and iron-clad floating and land batteries. In the attack on Fort Sumter, in 1861, these war appliances were first used in the United States. When I arrived at Charleston, in March of that year, to assume command of the forces there assembling and direct the attack on Fort Sumter, I found under construction a rough floating battery made of palmetto logs, under the direction of Captain Hamilton, an ex-United States naval officer. He intended to plate it with several sheets of rolled iron, each about three-quarters of an inch thick, and to arm it with four 32-pounder carronades. He and his battery were so much ridiculed, however, by the State government. He came to me in great discouragement, and expressed in vivid terms his certainty of success, and of revolutionizing future naval warfare as well as the construction of war vessels. I approved of Captain Hamilton's design, and having secured the necessary means, instructed him to finish his battery at the earliest moment practicable. This being accomplished before the attack on Fort Sumter opened, early in April I placed the floating battery in position at the western extremity of Sullivan's Island to enfilade certain barbette guns of the fort which could not be reached effectively by our land batteries. It therefore played an important part in that brief drama of thirty-three hours, receiving many shots without any serious injury. About one year later, in Hampton Roads, the *Virginia*, plated and roofed with two layers of railroad iron, met the *Monitor* in a momentous encounter, which first attracted the attention of the civilized world to the important change that iron-plating or "armors" would thenceforth create in naval architecture and armaments. The one and a half to two-inch plating used on Captain Hamilton's floating battery has already grown to about twelve inches thickness of steel plates of the best quality, but together with the utmost care, in the effort to resist the heaviest rifle-shots now used. About the same time that Captain Hamilton was constructing his floating battery, Mr. C. H. Steven, of Charleston, (who afterward died a brigadier-general at the battle of Chickamauga), commenced building an iron-clad land battery at Cumming's Point, the northern extremity of Morris Island and the point nearest to Fort Sumter—that is, about thirteen hundred years distant. This battery was to be built of heavy timbers covered with one layer of railroad iron, the rails well-fitted into each other, presenting an inclined, smooth surface of about thirty-fire degrees to the fire of Sumter; the surface was to be well greased and the guns were to fire through small embrasures supplied with strong iron shutters. I approved also of the plan, making such suggestions as my experience as an engineer warranted. This battery took an active part in the attack and was struck several times; but excepting the jamming and disabling one of the shutters, the battery remained uninjured to the end of the fight.

From Cumming's Point also, and in the same attack, was used the first rifled cannon fired in America. The day before I received orders from the Confederate Government, at Montgomery, to demand the evacuation or surrender of Fort Sumter, a vessel from England arriving in the outer harbor, signaled that she had something important for the Governor of the State. I sent out a harbor boat, which returned with a small Blakely rifled-gun, of two and a half inches diameter, with only fifty rounds of ammunition. I placed it at once behind a sand-bag parapet next to the Steven battery, where it did opportune service with its ten-pound shell while the ammunition lasted. The penetration of the projectiles into the brick masonry of the fort was not great at that distance, but the piece had great accuracy, and several of the shells entered the embrasures facing Morris Island. One of the officers of the garrison remarked after the surrender, that when they first heard the singular whizzing, screeching sound of the projectile, they did not understand its cause until one of the unexploded shells being found in the fort the mystery was solved. As a proof of the rapid strides taken by the artillery arm of the service, I shall mention that two years later the Federals fired against Fort Sumter, from nearly the same spot, rifle projectiles weighing three hundred pounds. Meantime I had received from England two other Blakely rifled cannon of thirteen and a quarter inches calibre. These magnificent specimens of heavy ordnance were, apart from their immense size, different in construction from any thing I had ever seen. They had been bored through from muzzle to breech; the breech was then plugged with a brass block extending into the bore at least two feet, and into which had been reamed a chamber about eighteen inches in length and six in diameter, while the vent entered the bore immediately in advance of this chamber. The projectiles provided were shells weighing, when loaded, about three hundred and fifty pounds, and solid cylindrical shots weighing seven hundred and thirty pounds; the charge for the latter was sixty pounds of powder. The first of these guns received was mounted in a battery specially constructed for it at "The Battery," at the immediate mouth of Cooper river, to command the inner harbor. As no instructions for their service accompanied the guns, and the metal between the exterior surface of the breech and the rear of the inner chamber did not exceed six to eight inches, against all experience in ordnance, apprehensions were excited that the gun would burst in firing with so large a charge and such weight of projectile. Under the circumstances it was determined to charge it with an empty shell and the minimum of powder necessary to move it; the charge was divided in two cartridges, one to fit the small rear chamber and the other the main bore. The gun was fired by means of a long lanyard from the bomb-proof attached to the battery; and, as apprehended it burst at the first fire, even with the relatively small charge used; the brass plug was found started back at least the sixteenth of an inch, splitting the breech with three of four cracks and rendering it useless.

With such a result I did not attempt, of course, to mount and use the other, but assembled a board of officers to study the principle that might be involved in the peculiar construction, and to make experiments generally with ordnance. The happy results of the extensive experiments made by this board with many guns of different caliber, including muskets, and last of all with the other Blakely, was that if the cartridge were not pressed down to the bottom of the bore of a gun, and a space were thus left in rear of the charge, as great a velocity could be imparted to the projectile with a much smaller charge and the gun was subject to less abrupt strain from the explosion, because this air-chamber, affording certain room for the expansion of the gases, gave time for the inertia of the heavy mass of the projectile to be overcome before the full explosion of the charge, and opportunity was also give for the ignition of the entire charge, so that no powder was wasted as in ordinary gunnery. When this was discovered the remaining Blakely was tried from a skid, without any cartridge in the rear chamber. It fired both projectiles, shell and solid shot, with complete success, notwithstanding the small amount of metal at the extremity of the breech. I at once utilized this discovery. We had a number of 8-inch Columbiads (remaining in Charleston after the capture of Sumter in 1861) which contained a powder-chamber of smaller diameter than the caliber of the gun. The vent in rear of this powder-chambers, leaving the latter to serve as an air-chamber, as in our use of the Blakely gun. They were then rifled and banded, and thus turned into admirable guns, which were effectively employed against the Federal iron-clads. I am surprised that the new principle adapted to these guns has not been used for the heavy ordnance of the present day, as it would secure great economy in weight and cost. The injured Blakely gun was subsequently thoroughly repaired, and made as efficient as when first received.

In the year 1854, while in charge as engineer of the fortifications of Louisiana, I attended a target practice with heavy guns by the garrison of Fort Jackson, on the Mississippi River, the object fired at being a hogshead floating with the current at the rate of about four and a half miles an hour. I was struck with the defaults of trailing or traversing the guns—42-pounders and 8-inch Columbiads—and with the consequent inaccuracy of the firing. Reflecting upon the matter, I devised soon afterward a simple method of overcoming the difficulty by the application of a "rack and lever" to the wheels of the chassis of the guns; and I sent drawings of the improvement to the Chief of Engineers, General Totten, who referred them, with his approval, to the Chief of Ordnance. In the course of a few weeks the latter informed me that his department had not yet noticed any great obstacle in traversing guns on moving objects, and therefore declined to adopt my invention. When charged in 1861 with the Confederate attack on Fort Sumter, I described this device to several of my engineer and artillery officers; but before I could have it applied I was ordered to Virginia to assume command of the Confederate force then assembling at Manassas. Afterward, on my return to Charleston in 1862, one of my artillery officers, Lieutenant-Colonel Yates, an intelligent and zealous soldier, applied this principle (modified, however) to one of the heavy guns in the harbor with such satisfactory results that I gave him orders to apply it is rapidly as possible to all guns of that class which we then had mounted. By April 6, 1863, when Admiral Dupont made his attack on Fort Sumter with seven monitors, the *New Ironsides*, several gunboats and mortal boats, our heaviest pieces had this traversing apparatus adapted to their chassis, and the result realized fully our expectations. However slow or fast the Federal vessels moved in their evolutions, they received a steady and unerring fire, which at first disconcerted them, and at last gave us a brilliant victory—disabling fire of the monitors, one of which, the *Keokuk*, sunk at her anchors that night. It is pertinent for me professionally to remark that had this Federal naval attack on Fort Sumter of the 6th of April, 1863, been made at night, while the fleet could have easily approached near enough to see the fort—a large, lofty object, covering several acres—the monitors, which were relatively so small and low on the water, could not have been seen from the fort. It would have been impossible, therefore, for the latter to have returned with any accuracy the fire of the fleet, and this plan of attack could have crumbled under the enormous missiles, which made holes two and a half feet deep in the walls, and shattered the latter in an alarming manner. I could not then have repaired during the day the damages of the night, and I am confident now, as I was then, that Fort Sumter, if thus attacked, must have been disabled and silenced in a few days. Such a result at that time would have been necessarily followed by the evacuation of Morris and Sullivan's Islands, and, soon after, of Charleston itself, for I had not yet had time to complete and arm the system of works, including James Island and the inner harbor, which enabled us six months later to bid defiance to Admiral Dahlgren's powerful fleet and Gilmore's strong land forces.

Notes

Chapter 1

The Infernal Device

1. ———, *Official Records of the Union and Confederate Navies in the War of the Rebellion*, ser. 1, vol. 4 (Washington, D.C.: Government Printing Office, 1884–1927), p. 567.

2. David Bushnell, Letter to Thomas Jefferson, October 1787, Washington: Manuscript Division, Library of Congress.

3. Diana Fontaine Corbin, *A Life of Matthew Fontaine Maury* (London: S. Low, Marston, Searle, & Rivington, 1888), p. 192.

4. Milton F. Perry, *Infernal Machines* (Baton Rouge: Louisiana State University Press, 1965), pp. 5–6.

5. Richard L. Maury, "The First Marine Torpedoes," *Southern Historical Society Papers*, vol. 31, 1903, p. 327.

6. Perry, p. 6.

7. Betty H. Maury, Personal Diary, Washington: Maury Papers, Manuscript Division, Library of Congress, July 10, 1861, entry.

8. Ibid.

9. ORN, ser. 1, vol. 6, p. 26.

10. Ibid., p. 304a.

11. Ibid., pp. 304a–304b.

12. Louis M. Goldsborough, letter to Secretary Welles dated October 17, 1861, Record Group 45, entry 81, National Archives.

Chapter 2

Captain Lee's Spar Torpedo Ram

1. P. G. T. Beauregard, "Torpedo Service in the Harbor and Water Defenses of Charleston," *Southern Historical Society papers*, vol. 5, April 1878, p. 145.

2. Louis S. Schaffer, *Confederate Underwater Warfare* (Jefferson: McFarland & Company, Inc., 1996), p. 82.

3. Beauregard, p. 147.

4. Ibid.

5. ———, *The War of the Rebellion: A Compilation of the Official Records of the Union and Confederate Armies,"* ser. 1, vol. 14 (Washington, D.C.: Government Printing Office), p. 631.

6. OR, ser. 1, vol. 14, p. 636.
7. Ibid., p. 637.
8. Ibid., pp. 648–49.
9. Ibid., pp. 670–71.
10. Ibid.
11. Ibid., pp. 671–72.
12. Ibid.
13. Ibid., pp. 694, 719.
14. Milton F. Perry, *Infernal Machines* (Baton Rouge: Louisiana State University Press, 1965), p. 60.
15. OR, ser. 1, vol. 14, p. 1017.
16. Ibid., pp. 817–18.
17. Ibid., p. 907.
18. Ibid., p. 918.

CHAPTER 3
ROWBOATS AT WAR

1. _____, *Official Records of the Union and Confederate Navies in the War of the Rebellion*, ser. 1, vol. 13 (Washington, D.C.: Government Printing Office, 1884–1927), pp. 820–21.
2. _____, *The War of the Rebellion: A Compilation of the Official Records of the Union and Confederate Armies,"* ser. 1, vol. 14 (Washington: Government Printing Office), p. 791.
3. OR, ser. 1, vol. 14, p. 820.
4. William T. Glassell, "Reminiscences of Torpedo Service in Charleston Harbor," *Southern Historical Society Papers,* 1877, vol. 4, p. 226.
5. J. Thomas Scharf, *History of the Confederate States Navy* (New York: Crown Publishers Inc., 1877), p. 754.
6. Ibid.
7. Ibid., p. 227.
8. Ibid., pp. 227–28.
9. ORN, ser. 1, vol. 13, p. 821.
10. William H. Parker, *Recollections of a Naval Officer*, New York: Charles Scribners' Sons, 1883, p. 333.
11. Ibid., p. 327.
12. Ibid., p. 333.
13. Scharf, pp. 689–90.
14. Ibid., p. 690.
15. Ibid.
16. Parker, p. 335.
17. OR, ser. 1, vol. 14, p. 907.
18. Scharf, p. 693.

CHAPTER 4
THE CSS *TORCH*

1. _____, *The War of the Rebellion: A Compilation of the Official Records of the Union and Confederate Armies,"* ser. 1, vol. 28, pt. 2 (Washington: Government Printing Office), p. 229.
2. Ibid.
3. OR, ser. 1, vol. 14, pp. 965–66.

4. Milton F. Perry, *Infernal Machines* (Baton Rouge: Louisiana State University Press, 1965), pp. 77–78.

5. OR, ser. 1, vol. 28, pt. 2, p. 251.

6. Ibid., p. 254.

7. W. P. Poulnot, "Rebel Ram," *Charleston News and Courier*, December 20, 1895.

8. OR, ser. 1, vol. 14, pp. 498–99.

9. Poulnot, December 1895.

10. OR, ser. 1, vol. 28, pt. 2, p. 498.

11. Ibid., p. 500.

CHAPTER 5

DAVID AND GOLIATH

1. E. Milby Burton, *The Siege of Charleston 1861–1865* (Columbia: University of South Carolina Press, 1970), p. 218.

2. David C. Ebaugh, "David C. Ebaugh on the Building of the David," *South Carolina Magazine*, January 1953, p. 23.

3. Ibid.

3. James H. Tomb, "Submarines and Torpedo Boats, CSN," *Confederate Veteran*, April 1914, p. 168.

5. William T. Glassell, "Reminiscences of Torpedo Service in Charleston Harbor," *Southern Historical Society Papers,* 1877, vol. 4, p. 230.

6. Ibid., pp. 230–31.

7. Ibid., p. 231.

8. Ibid.

9. John Johnson, *The Defense of Charleston Harbor* (Charleston: Walker, Evans, & Cogswell Co., 1890), pp. xxx–xxxi.

10. Tomb, p. 168.

11. Glassell, p. 232.

12. ———, *Official Records of the Union and Confederate Navies in the War of the Rebellion*, ser. 1, vol. 15 (Washington, D.C.: Government Printing Office, 1884–1927), p. 12.

13. ORN, ser. 1, vol. 15, p. 16.

14. Perry, pp. 85–86.

15. Ibid., p. 84.

16. J. Thomas Scharf, *History of the Confederate States Navy* (New York: Crown Publishers, Inc., 1887), p. 754.

17. ORN, ser. 1, vol. 15, p. 12.

CHAPTER 6

THE "DAVID" CLASS TORPEDO BOATS

1. ———, *Official Records of the Union and Confederate Navies in the War of the Rebellion*, ser. 1, vol. 15 (Washington, D.C.: Government Printing Office, 1884–1927), p. 29.

2. Ibid.

3. Ibid., p. 30.

4. Ibid., p. 48.

5. Ibid., p. 64.

6. Ibid., ser. 1, vol. 28, pt. 2, p. 421.

7. Ibid.

8. Ibid., p. 442.

9. Ibid., p. 504.
10. Ibid.
11. Ibid., pp. 595–97.
12. Ibid., pp. 538, 548.
13. ORN, ser. 1, vol. 15, pp. 334–35.
14. Milton F. Perry, *Infernal Machines* (Baton Rouge: Louisiana State University Press, 1965), pp. 122–23.
15. ORN, ser. 1, vol. 15, pp. 358–59.
16. Ibid.
17. Ibid., vol. 9, p. 561.
18. Ibid., vol. 15, p. 397.
19. Ibid., p. 405.
20. James H. Tomb, "Submarines and Torpedo Boats," *Confederate Veteran*, April 1914, p. 168.
21. OR, ser. 1, vol. 35, pt. 2, p. 460.
22. Ibid.
23. ORN, ser. 1, vol. 15, p. 678.
24. Ibid., ser. 1, vol. 16, p. 15.
25. Ibid., p. 460.
26. Ibid., ser. 1, vol. 21, p. 187.
27. Ibid., vol. 21, pp. 902–3.
28. Ibid., ser. 1, vol. 22, pp. 267–68.
29. Ibid., p. 269.

CHAPTER 7

THE CSS *SQUIB*

1. William S. Dudley, *Going South: U.S. Navy Officer Resignations & Dismissals on the Eve of the Civil War* (Washington: Naval Historical Foundation, 1981), p. 40.
2. R. Thomas Campbell, *Gray Thunder, Exploits of the Confederate States Navy* (Shippensburg: White Mane Publishing Company, Inc., 1996), p. 36.
3. ———, *Official Records of the Union and Confederate Navies in the War of the Rebellion*, ser. 1, vol. 7 (Washington, D.C.: Government Printing Office, 1884–1927), pp. 46–48.
4. Ibid., p. 546.
5. Dunbar Rowland, *Jefferson Davis, His Letters, Papers and Speeches*, vol. 7 (Jackson: 1923), p. 109.
6. Hunter Davidson, "Electrical Torpedoes as a System of Defence," *Southern Historical Society Papers*, vol. 2, July 1876, p. 2.
7. J. Thomas Scharf, *History of the Confederate States Navy* (New York: Crown Publishers, Inc., 1887), p. 728.
8. ORN, ser. 1, vol. 9, p. 601.
9. William H. Parker, *Recollections of a Naval Officer* (New York: Charles Scribners' Sons, 1883), p. 350.
10. Robert Holcombe, "Types of Ships," *The Confederate Navy, the Ships, Men and Organization, 1861–65* (Annapolis: Naval Institute Press, 1997), p. 62.
11. R. O. Cowley, "The Confederate Torpedo Service," *Century Magazine*, vol. 56, June 1898, p. 297.
12. Milton F. Perry, *Infernal Machines* (Baton Rouge: Louisiana State University Press, 1965), pp. 125–26.
13. ORN, ser. 1, vol. 9, p. 604.

14. Perry, p. 126.
15. Cowley, p. 297.
16. John M. Coski, *Capital Navy* (Campbell: Savas Woodbury Publishers, 1996), p. 126.
17. ORN, ser. 1, vol. 9, p. 603.
18. Davidson, p. 4.
19. ORN, ser. 1, vol. 9, p. 626.
20. Perry, p. 128.
21. Edwin L. Combs, *On Duty at Wilmington: The Confederate Navy on the Cape Fear River* (Greenville: Master's Thesis, East Carolina University, 1996), p. 128.
22. ORN, ser. 1, vol. 2, p. 754.

CHAPTER 8

THE "SQUIB" CLASS TORPEDO BOATS

1. ———, *Official Records of the Union and Confederate Navies in the War of the Rebellion*, ser. 1, vol. 19 (Washington, D.C.: Government Printing Office, 1884–1927), pp. 631–32.
2. Ibid., ser. 1, vol. 20, pp. 690–91.
3. Ibid., ser. 1, vol. 21, p. 106.
4. ORN, ser. 2, vol. 2, pp. 750–51.
5. Ibid., ser. 1, vol. 11, p. 707.
6. Charles L. Dufour, *Nine Men in Gray* (Garden City: Doubleday & Company, Inc., 1963), p. 150.
7. ORN, ser. 1, vol. 11, p. 797.
8. Dufour, p. 150.
9. ORN, ser. 1, vol. 11, pp. 797–98.
10. Ibid., p. 798.
11. Ibid., p. 803.
12. Ibid.
13. Ibid., p. 804.
14. ———, *Civil War Naval Chronology* (Washington: Naval History Division, Navy Department, 1971), pp. 252, 299, 322.
15. Ibid., p. 632.
16. Ibid., pp. 683–84.
17. Ibid.
18. Dufour, p. 152.
19. Edwin L. Combs, *On Duty at Wilmington, The Confederate Navy on the Cape Fear River* (Master's Thesis, East Carolina University, June 1996), pp. 101–2.
20. ORN, ser. 2, vol. 2, pp. 688–89.
21. Ibid., pp. 790–91.
22. Ibid., p. 683.
23. Maxine Turner, *Navy Gray* (Tuscaloosa: The University of Alabama Press, 1988), pp. 233–34.

CHAPTER 9

A DESPERATE MISSION

1. Ralph W. Donnelly, "A Confederate Navy Forlorn Hope," *Military Affairs*, Summer 1964, p. 73.
2. ———, *Official Records of the Union and Confederate Navies in the War of the Rebellion*, ser. 1, vol. 11 (Washington, D.C.: Government Printing Office, 1884–1927), pp. 811–12.

   3. W. F. Shippey, "A Leaf From My Logbook," *Southern Historical Society Papers*, vol. 12, 1884, p. 417.
   4. Charles L. Dufour, *Nine Men in Gray* (Garden City: Doubleday & Company, Inc., 1963), p. 152.
   5. Shippey, p. 418.
   6. Ibid.
   7. Ibid., pp. 418–19.
   8. Donnelly, p. 76.
   9. Shippey, p. 419.
  10. Donnelly, p. 76.
  11. Shippey, p. 419.
  12. Donnelly, p. 77.
  13. Shippey, p. 420.
  14. Ibid.
  15. Donnelly, p. 77.
  16. Shippey, pp. 420–21.
  17. Ibid., p. 421.

Afterword

   1. ———, *Official Records of the Union and Confederate Navies in the War of the Rebellion*, ser. 1, vol. 11 (Washington, D.C.: Government Printing Office, 1884–1927), pp. 378–79.
   2. Maxine Turner, *Navy Gray* (Tuscaloosa: The University of Alabama Press, 1988), pp. 244–45.
   3. Milton F. Perry, *Infernal Machines* (Baton Rouge: Louisiana State University Press, 1965), pp. 191–92.
   4. ORN, ser. 1, vol. 3, pp. 732–34.
   5. David P. Werlich, *Admiral of the Amazon* (Charlottesville: University Press of Virginia, 1990), p. 105.
   6. Richard N. Current, *Encyclopedia of the Confederacy* (New York: Simone & Schuster, 1993), pp. 447–48.
   7. Perry, p. 194.
   8. Current, p. 150.
   9. Perry, p. 193.
  10. ———, *Confederate Veteran*, vol. 37, July 1929, p. 266.
  11. ORN, ser. 1, vol. 28, pt. 2, p. 504.

BIBLIOGRAPHY

———.   *Confederate Veteran*, vol. 37, July 1929.

———.   *Civil War Naval Chronology*. Washington: Naval History Division, Navy Department, 1971.

———.   *Official Records of the Union and Confederate Navies in the War of the Rebellion.* Washington, D.C.: Government Printing Office, 1884–1927.

———.   *The War of the Rebellion: A Compilation of the Official Records of the Union and Confederate Armies.* Washington, D.C.: Government Printing Office, ser. 1, vol. 14.

Beauregard, P. G. T.   "Torpedo Service in the Harbor and Water Defenses of Charleston." *Southern Historical Society Papers*, vol. 5 (April 1878).

Burton, E. Milby   *The Siege of Charleston 1861–1865.* Columbia: University of South Carolina Press, 1970.

Bushnell, David   Letter to Thomas Jefferson, October 1787. Washington: Manuscript Division, Library of Congress.

Campbell, R. Thomas   *Gray Thunder, Exploits of the Confederate States Navy.* Shippensburg: White Mane Publishing Company, Inc., 1996.

Campbell, R. Thomas   *The CSS H. L. Hunley.* Shippensburg: White Mane Publishing Company, Inc., 1999.

Combs, Edwin L.   *On Duty at Wilmington: The Confederate Navy on the Cape Fear River.* Greenville: Master's Thesis, East Carolina University, 1996.

Corbin, Diana Fontain   *A Life of Matthew Fontaine Maury.* London: S. Low, Marston, Searle, & Rivington, 1888.

Coski, John M.   *Capital Navy.* Campbell: Savas Woodbury Publishers, 1996.

Cowley, R. O.   "The Confederate Torpedo Service." *Century Magazine,* vol. 56 (June 1898).

Current, Richard N.   *Encyclopedia of the Confederacy.* New York: Simon & Schuster, 1993.

Davidson, Hunter   "Electrical Torpedoes as a System of Defence." *Southern Historical Society Papers,* vol. 2 (Richmond: July 1876).

Donnelly, Ralph W.   "A Confederate Navy Forlorn Hope." *Military Affairs* (Summer 1964).

Donnelly, Ralph W.   *The Confederate States Marine Corps.* Shippensburg: White Mane Publishing Company, Inc., 1989.

Dudley, William S.   *Going South: U.S. Navy Officer Resignations & Dismissals on the Eve of the Civil War.* Washington, D.C.: Naval Historical Foundation, 1981.

Dufour, Charles L.   *Nine Men in Gray.* Garden City: Doubleday & Company, Inc., 1963.

Durkin, Joseph T.   *Confederate Navy Chief: Stephen R. Mallory.* Chapel Hill: The University of North Carolina Press, 1954.

Ebaugh, David C.   "David C. Ebaugh on the Building of the David." *South Carolina Magazine* (January 1953).

Glassell, William T.   "Reminiscences of Torpedo Service in Charleston Harbor." *Southern Historical Society Papers,* vol. 4 (1877).

Goldsborough, Louis M.   Letter to Secretary Welles. National Archives, October 17, 1861, Record Group 45, entry 81.

Holcombe, Robert   "Types of Ships." *The Confederate Navy, the Ships, Men and Organization, 1861–65.* Annapolis: Naval Institute Press, 1997.

Johnson, John   *The Defense of Charleston Harbor*. Charleston: Walker, Evans & Cogswell Co., Publishers, 1890.

Jones, Virgil C.   *The Civil War at Sea*. 3 vols. New York: Holt, Rinehart, and Winston, 1960–1962.

Luraghi, Raimondo   *A History of the Confederate Navy*. Annapolis: Naval Institute Press, 1996.

Maury, Betty H.   Personal Diary. Washington: Maury Papers, Manuscript Division, Library of Congress, July 10, 1861.

Maury, Richard L.   "The First Marine Torpedoes." *Southern Historical Society Papers*, vol. 31 (1903).

Parker, William H.   *Recollections of a Naval Officer*. New York: Charles Scribners' Sons, 1883.

Perry, Milton F.   *Infernal Machines*. Baton Rouge: Louisiana State University Press, 1965.

Poulnot, W. P.   "Rebel Ram." *Charleston News and Courier* (December 20, 1895).

Read, Charles W.   "Reminiscences of the Confederate States Navy." *Southern Historical Society Papers*, vol. 1 (May 1876).

Robinson, William Morrison, Jr.   *The Confederate Privateers*. New Haven: Yale University Press, 1928.

Rosen, Robert N.   *Confederate Charleston*. Columbia: The University of South Carolina Press, 1994.

Rowland, Dunbar   *Jefferson Davis, his Letters, Papers and Speeches*. Jackson: 1923, vol. 7.

Schaffer, Louis S.   *Confederate Underwater Warfare*. Jefferson: McFarland & Company, Inc., 1996.

Scharf, J. Thomas   *History of the Confederate States Navy*. New York: Crown Publishers Inc., 1877.

Shippey, W. F.   "A Leaf From My Logbook." *Southern Historical Society Papers*, vol. 12 (1884).

Silverstone, Paul H.   *Warships of the Civil War Navies*. Annapolis: Naval Institute Press, 1989.

Spencer, William F.   *The Confederate Navy in Europe*. Tuscaloosa: The University of Alabama Press, 1983.

Stanton, C. L.

"Submarines and Torpedo Boats." *Confederate Veteran* (September 1914).

Stern, Philip Van Doren

The Confederate Navy, A Pictorial History. New York: Bonanza Books, 1962.

Still, William N., Jr.

Confederate Shipbuilding. Columbia: University of South Carolina Press, 1987.

Tomb, James H.

"Submarines and Torpedo Boats, CSN." *Confederate Veteran* (April 1914).

Turner, Maxine

Navy Gray. Tuscaloosa: The University of Alabama Press, 1988.

Von Sheliha, Victor E. R.

A Treatise on Coast Defence. London: 1868.

Wells, Tom Henderson

The Confederate Navy, A Study in Organization. Tuscaloosa: The University of Alabama Press, 1971.

Werlich, David P.

Admiral of the Amazon. Charlottesville: University Press of Virginia, 1990.

Wise, Stephen R.

Lifeline of the Confederacy. Columbia: University of South Carolina Press, 1988.

INDEX

Blank

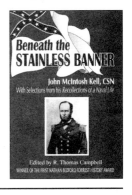

— Award Winning Author —
Winner of the 1997 Nathan Bedford Forrest History Award

R. THOMAS CAMPBELL has been studying and writing about the Confederate experience in the War Between the States for many years. He is a frequent contributor to *Confederate Veteran*, the magazine of the Sons of Confederate Veterans, of which he is a member, and also in the regional publications of that organization.

Mr. Campbell is a graduate of the Wharton School of Business and Finance at the University of Pennsylvania, and holds a Bachelor of Science degree from Villanova University. He is currently preparing additional studies of the activities of the Confederate Navy. Mr. Campbell resides in West Chester, Pennsylvania.

— Illustrations —

Front Cover
CSS *DAVID* STRIKES THE USS *NEW IRONSIDES*
Copyright © 1999 Graphic Courtesy of Daniel Dowdey

CAPTAIN FRANCIS D. LEE, CSA
Inventor and Advocate of the Star Torpedo
South Carolina Historical Society

Inside Front Cover
TORPEDO BOAT CSS *DAVID*
Joseph Hinds, Illustrator

Inside Back Cover
SQUIB CLASS TORPEDO BOAT
Copyright © 1999 Graphic Courtesy of Daniel Dowdey

WHITE MANE PUBLISHING CO., INC.

To Request a Catalog Please Write to:
WHITE MANE PUBLISHING COMPANY, INC.
P.O. Box 152 • Shippensburg, PA 17257
e-mail: marketing@whitemane.com